Over the Top and Back

Over the Top and Back

They Answered Their Country's Call

Edythe G. Dean

VANTAGE PRESS
New York

Excerpts from the *Ravenna Republican* and the *Kent Courier*, reports from World War I, 1917–1920, by Charles M. Conaway, are reprinted with permission of the *Kent-Ravenna Record-Courier*, successor to the aforementioned newspapers, as well as the letters from members of the community that were written "by the boys" from abroad.

Text researched by Harold T. Nading
Text edited by Edythe G. Nading Dean

Cover design by Susan Thomas

FIRST EDITION

Published by Vantage Press, Inc.
419 Park Ave. South, New York, NY 10016

Manufactured in the United States of America
ISBN: 0-533-15017-5

Library of Congress Catalog Card No.: 2004096262

0 9 8 7 6 5 4 3 2 1

To Arthur G. Brode, our uncle, and Ethel Brode, our mother.

Each served in their own way to make the world a better place in which to live.

Also, to Charles M. Conaway, who so faithfully reported on OUR BOYS for the benefit of history.

And to the men of Company C who answered the call to serve without hesitation.

Preface

These were OUR boys. They were the boys from Portage County who volunteered to go and fight to make the world free. This is their story. It will make you laugh and make you cry, but in the end, it will make you think, because of the sacrifice they made. They were the men of Company M. They would become Company C 136th Machine Gun Battalion, but to us they will always be OUR boys! May we never forget them.

It is also a poignant example of how newspapers write our history. I am convinced that nothing will ever replace the written word.

—E.G.D.

Acknowledgments

I wish to acknowledge the *Record-Courier* and Roger Di Paolo, editor, for allowing me to print this account of Ravenna's history. I hope everyone who reads it looks at this history as part of the history of America. The *Record-Courier* is successor to the *Kent Ravenna Courier* which was the successor to *Ravenna Republican.* Thanks so much!

I want to acknowledge my mother, Ethel Brode, who, while working in Washington, D.C., kept a record sent to her by her mother, Mrs. James Brode, of Charles M. Conaway's accounts of the war which is where I first read his writings. She kept those accounts because her brother, Arthur Brode, was serving with the Company C, 136th Machine Gun Battalion, 37th Division.

I wish to acknowledge my brother, Harold Nading, whose idea it was to expand those writings further into the account you read here. His relentless research brought these brave men to life.

I also wish to acknowledge all those who served and those who kept the home fires burning and waited for their sons to return, although some of them did not.

I want to thank my husband, Harold Dean, who listened to my accounts of this history and the endless phone calls with my brother and put up with my endless hours on the computer preparing this book.

I also want to thank the numerous people who listened to my stories of this Company and this war and encouraged me. Thank you so much!

And last, but mainly most important, many accolades to Charles M. Conaway for his accounts of these men who fought so bravely. He was truly the first embedded reporter, along with being a soldier.

About Charles M. Conaway

Charles M. Conaway spent fifty years as a reporter. He started as a linotype operator for the *Republican* at the age of fourteen. After he graduated from Ravenna High School he joined the *Republican* staff. Two years later, he enlisted in Ravenna's famed National Guard unit, Company M, which later became Company C, 136th Machine Gun Company, 37th Division, which distinguished itself on the battlefields of Belgium and France.

Mr. Conaway continued as a member of the Guard after WWI and was an officer in military intelligence in WWII, attaining the rank of captain.

Between wars he gained recognition as a top newspaperman, working not only for the *Republican* but also the *Alliance Review, Canton Repository,* and a paper in Iron River, Michigan, before joining the *Plain Dealer* where he served as a reporter and was eventually appointed the newspaper's Akron bureau chief, a post he held for twenty-six years until he resigned to publish the *Tallmadge Home News.*

In 1960 he joined the staff of the *Record-Courier* and covered City Hall in Ravenna.

He also served as a journalism instructor at Kent State University.

The accounts he wrote for the *Republican* were probably his first published writings as a reporter.

Over the Top and Back

The Ravenna Republican:
Monday, April 5, 1917
First Call to Arms Sounded in Ravenna

Patriotic Meeting of Citizens at Town Hall Saturday Evening. Seventy-five Men Needed for Ravenna's Regimental Quota—Everyone Invited to Attend

A meeting has been called for next Saturday evening at seven-thirty PM at the town hall for the purpose of securing enlistments for service in the 10th Ohio Volunteer Infantry for three years. Should the war be ended before the expiration of the three years, the volunteers will receive their honorable discharge at that time.

This was the announcement made by Mr. E. D. Neikirk, who is now actively engaged, in cooperation with Major Love of Youngstown, to secure recruits.

Married men or men with others dependent on them will not be accepted.

The meeting will be announced by the ringing of the courthouse bell, which rang for the call to arms in 1861.

Everyone is invited to attend the meeting. Women are especially invited to attend.

The Ravenna Republican:
Monday, April 9, 1917
Real Patriotism Evident in Saturday
Evening Meeting

Thirty-seven Young Men Volunteer Their Services for the Cause of Country and Sign Enlistment Roll—Rousing Addresses by W. J. Beckley, Kingdon Siddall, H. R. Loomis, E. F. Robison and Civil War Veteran C. C. Webber—War Spirit Runs High

Three town halls would not have afforded more than comfortable accommodation for the crowd of citizens who assembled within the walls of the brick pile Saturday evening at the ringing of the courthouse bell. The object of the meeting was to secure enlistments for Ravenna's portion of the Portage county company to be organized as an integral part of the Tenth Regiment Ohio National Guards.

The meeting was called to order by Mayor Fred Byers, who presented attorney W. J. Beckley. He recapitulated the events of the week which culminated in a declaration of war with Germany. He then addressed himself to the need of the hour in the way of thorough preparation for the conflict ahead. He said that Americans everywhere can be depended upon to uphold the flag and among patriotic citizens none will be found truer than German-Americans who are among the best citizens of the Republic and can be depended upon to stand by its institutions and uphold its liberties, which they came here to enjoy. He made an appeal for volunteer enlistments, urging that Ravenna show its readiness to meet the demands of the hour. "The quicker and better the preparation, the sooner will the war be over and the future peace of the world be placed on a surer and firmer foundation," he said.

He was followed by Kingdon Siddall, son of attorney I. T. Siddall, who explained the nature of the service and talked of the duty which all citizens owe to their land and the government under which they live. Mr. Siddall is a member of Troop A—U.S.A. and was at the Mexican border in the early days of the threatened rupture between that country and this one. He spoke of the training given those who enlist and of its value, not only in a physical sense, but in building up a firmer and appreciative spirit of liberty, a spirit that looks out for every phase of its development and is more intelligently alive to the great responsibilities of citizenship.

E. D. Neikirk then made a brief talk explanatory of service. A Portage county company will be maintained as a unit and elect its own officers. When the draft comes, the Portage county boys will have to go anyway and will be apportioned among other companies all over the country.

C. C. Webber, a civil war veteran, was then called to the platform and speaking from an experience that covered four years and three and one half months of that great conflict, he said that during that period, which had its trials, hardships and severe disciplines as well as its enjoyable features, he never felt better in his life. The discipline and the stamina developed by its regimen were worth all the sacrifices. "You are going to do things worthwhile and you will be given opportunity to prove the best there is in you, things that will rejoice your American hearts," he said. Pointing to the big flag at the rear of the platform, he said, "Don't ever let that flag touch the ground," sentiment that brought out cheers. Mr. Weber served as a color bearer and told of one battle in which the flag bearer was shot down, but before the emblem could fall to the ground, it was caught up by eager hands that kept it continually aloft. He exhorted the young men not to be afraid to enlist or hesitate. "You will never regret it," he said. "It is volunteers that the country wants, not conscripts."

H. R. Loomis followed Mr. Webber and first warned his listeners that Germany has counted the cost of entering this conflict with the United States and there is an idea in the land of the Kaiser that Americans will exert all their energies to participate in the battles of trade and commerce but will not fight with the sword. "The greatest shock we can give the Germans is to show them this is not true and prove it by making the war one of tremendous initiative and fight with all our might and vigor from the start. If we do this," he said, "we will make an early peace so much the surer. By so doing we keep up the spirit of the army and of the navy. When we show Germany this is a UNITED country and we are entering the conflict with all our might because we know it is a battle between free Republican government in which the people decide policies, dictate military programs and that of monarchial military aristocracy in the affairs of which people have no voice and no choice save to fight when told to do so by their masters." He warned against the idea this is necessarily going to be a short war. "We hope that such will be the case, but we cannot tell," and warned of what the country paid in 1861 when it refused to take the Rebellion seriously. "If we marshall all our resources: agricultural, industrial and mechanical, and raise an army and navy commensurate with the demands of the hour, we shall materially shorten the duration of the conflict. The greatest danger will be in the next six months," he said. "If we take immediate and hearty hold of the situation and show Germany the deadly certainty with which we intend to strike swiftly, unitedly, and tremendously, we shall ensure the future and hasten the day when autocratic governments like that of the Kaiser will disappear forever from the Earth.

"It has been said by countries governed by crowned heads that republics cannot successfully defend themselves; that a strong central authority is necessary, a power above and entirely independent of the people that tells them when they must fight and when they may pursue peace. Are we going to make good and refute this doctrine of the crowned heads that rule by 'the divine right of kings?' If we fail, it will be because we are too much given to luxury. Let us start in right and put Portage county in the roll of honor by furnishing a company of volunteer soldiers."

The speaker spoke of the importance of marshalling all of our resources for the successful prosecution of the war. He reminded his hearers that Portage county is not an industrial county but an agricultural one. He believed that there should be an organization of farmers in every township for the purpose of growing more food stuffs. Plow more land, raise more grain. These two items are important. The fact that so many roads in the county are improved is a great helping factor. Let Portage county come promptly to the front and not only furnish its quota of men, but of grain and other provisions.

4

Judge E. F. Robison then made a short talk in which he said that he was loath to see a state of war, but now that it had come he believed the nation and every unit of the nation should go after it with might and main. The greater danger is in overconfidence. "We must PREPARE," he said, "by getting busy along all lines."

The meeting was opened by the singing of "America" and at the close of speeches, three rousing cheers were given for those who had already enlisted.

Calls for volunteers were then made and after the evening thirty-seven young men had signed the enlistment roll, including Will Horne, 24; John R. Byers, 22; Harold Hubbell, 23; David Murphy, 20; Charles A. Cope, 30; Floyd Chambers, 24; George Parsons, 20; Clark Abel, 18; William Trexler, 20; Chester Frank, 22; Frank Elgin, 20; Joseph Cole, 19; Roy Jones, 20; Alfred Alexander, 16; Harold Robinson, 17; Emmett Goodyear, 17; Willis Moore, 22; Hubert E. Thompson, 18; H. Harold Mott, 23; William F. Gray, 20; Clarence Gray, 17; Archie M. Robertson, 21; John Lock, 22; John Morgan, 21; Emerson R. Kreible, 18; Nick Jenson, 21; Claire Dunning; Frank Szekula, 18; Walter J. Keeter; Joseph Carter; Tony Ruggieri, 22; Harold A. Anderson; Henry Montigney, 22; Lewis Blieu, 32; Charles Conaway. Meetings will be held in other parts of the county until the full quota of 150 men has been secured. When the Regiment has been fully manned, the boys will go to Cedar Point where they will be equipped and drilled.

Courthouse Bell Announces War

Same Bell That Rang the News of
Ft. Sumter and the Secession

The ringing of the courthouse bell on Friday afternoon announced to the people of Ravenna the momentous fact that Congress and President Wilson has taken the final step that placed this government and people in a state of war with Germany. War came at 1:13 PM when President Wilson signed the war resolution passed by Congress. He immediately issued a call for volunteers for the army and navy and a proclamation to the nation.

In his proclamation, the president gave strong warning to "alien enemies" of the United States living within the borders of this country that they will be drastically dealt with should they attempt to set affoot any conspiracy or intrigue against the United States. Unnaturalized Germans are forbidden to carry any arms within the boundaries of the nation, and are forbidden to agitate against the government of the United States or the officers, and are also cautioned not to approach within a half mile of any fortification or military establishment.

Simultaneously with the ringing of the historic courthouse bell—the bell that sounded the tocsin of war with the States of the Secession and four years later tolled the sad news of the assassination of the immortal Lincoln, the flag of the nation was unfurled from the steel staff in front of the temple of justice, to remain daily as long as the country is engaged in the conflict. At the same time hundreds of homes displayed the stars and stripes, while citizens hastened to adorn their persons with miniature emblems of the Republic. A quiet spirit of patriotism that stands ready to uphold the flag and all it stands for.

The Ravenna Republican:
Thursday, April 12, 1917
War Enlistments Still Going On

Meeting Will Be Held in Different Parts of the County—Good Results

Arthur Diezman of South Prospect Street, 19; Ray Long of Mechanic Street, 20; and Francis Moncey of Vine Street, 18; have added their names to the roll of volunteer soldiers who will be enrolled into a Portage county company for the 10th Regiment, Ohio National Guard. This makes Ravenna's total forty, up to date to which Mantua added one on Tuesday evening, making a grand total of forty-one. The boys are enthusiastic over the prospect of being able to serve their country.

Another meeting will be held in Ravenna this Thursday evening, at which the recruits will be put through the drill by former chief gunner, Charles Cope, who will be assisted by Sergeant Hoff of Company F., 2nd, Missouri National Guards. Additional enlistments will be received at this meeting and at all future meetings in the county.

A well-attended meeting was held in Mantua Tuesday evening, at which a stirring address was made by attorney S. F. Hanselman of this city. At the close of the meeting, Mr. Turner, one of Mantua's young men, signed the petition, being the first recruit from that town.

E. D. Neikirk and Harold L. Hubbell, Ravenna organizers, were in Garrettsville this week and found promising prospects for a satisfactory number of enlistments at that model village.

Seventy-five names must first be secured before the petition can be filed with the governor. Of this number, at least sixty-five men must be able to stand the physical examination, this number being the peace strength of a company. The war strength is about 138, and it is planned to secure a minimum of 150 enlistments so to place Portage county in the front ranks of military duty.

The Ravenna Republican:
Thursday, April 22, 1917
Ravenna Soldiers to Be Mustered
in Saturday Eve

Thirty Volunteers Examined and Accepted Up to Date—Enlistments and Examinations Still in Progress

Thirty volunteers have been examined and accepted for members of Portage county's company, 10th Regiment, Ohio National Guard and word was received today that the boys will be mustered to the service at Ravenna on Saturday evening.

First Lieutenant Earl W. Cliffe of Youngstown, who is conducting the examinations, is highly pleased with the results thus far.

Ravenna's HONOR ROLL consists of a grade and quality of men of which the city may well be proud.

The company is to be instituted next Saturday evening, April 28, at Ravenna, so those who wish to share the honors with the charter members will have to hustle and get their names on the roll. Enlisting and examinations are still in progress at the town hall where the officer in charge will be glad to answer any questions.

On Sunday evening the Company will assemble at the town hall at 7 PM and march in ranks to the First Methodist Episcopal church and listen to a patriotic address from the pastor, Rev. Charles H. Hauger.

Special seats will be reserved for the soldier boys and the service will be exclusively of a patriotic character.

The Roll of Honor

Raymond E. Long, Leon Muster, Wilbur C. Minnick, George Clark, Walter O. Moore, Emerson P. Krieble, Herbert E. Thompson,

Harold L. Hubbell, William H. Trexler, Clair S. Dunning, Nick James, Charles M. Conaway, William F. Horne, Joseph R. Cole, Charles Henry Baldwin, Arthur L. Diezman, Raymond A. Summers, H. Harold Mott, George W. Parsons, Lewis C. Blieu, Walter J. Keeter, Joe Ronato, Harold W. Andrews, William F. Gray, Alva B. Rice, Robert N. Yeend, Charles R. Cope, LeRoy Jones, Samuel Specht, Floyd J. Chambers. All of the above are Ravenna boys.

The Ravenna Republican:
Monday, April, 30, 1917
Portage Soldiers Mustered in and
Enlistments Still On

**Required Quota Passed and Local Company Now
Assured—Will Receive Additional Number Up to
100—Grand Rush to the Colors in Closing
Hours—Community Lauds Its Soldier Boys—Cash Fund
for Company**

The Roll of Honor

Anderson, Harold W.

Baldwin, Charles H.

Blieu, Lewis C.

Boyd, Lawrence S., Kent

Cannavino, Mark

Chambers, Floyd J.

Conaway, Charles M.

Cope, Charles R.

Davidson, George E.

De Angelis, Benjamin

Diezman, Arthur L.

Dustman, Dewey A.

Elgin, Frank W., Kent

George, Kennerdell E., Kent

Hallabaugh, Clifford F.

Haas, Kennith M., Kent

Jacobsen, Berger, H.

Jones, John H.

Keeter, Walter J.

Anderson, Melvin G.

Baxter, Clarence A.

Brode, Arthur G.

Byers, John R.

Carter, Joseph F.

Clark, George

Cole, Joseph R.

Creque, Charles G.

Damicon, Leo A.

Dickens, Frederick

Dunning, Clair S.

Dyer, Edward F.

Gray, William F.

Horne, William F.

Hubbell, Harold L.

Jackson, Wallace N.

James, Nicholas

Jones, LeRoy

Kick, Luther M.

Krieble, Emerson P.
Lackey, John W., Kent
Lindsay, Robert J.
Marsh, Shearold L.
McKeever, George W.
Miller, Maxwell M., Kent
Moon, George H., Kent
Myers, George W., Kent
Parsons, George W.
Puffer, Harry S.
Rice, Alva B.
Rock, John
Sawyer, Bennett, J., Kent
Simpson, Walter A., Kent
Specht, Samuel C.
Smith, William B.
Trexler, William H.

Knapp, James F.
Lauver, Roy B.
Long, Raymond E.
Marsh, Jesse L.
Minnich, Wilber C.
Moore, Walter O.
Mosier, Leon
Mott, Harold
Price, Earl C.
Renato, Joseph
Rufi, Joseph
Ruggiere, Tony
Skilton, William B.
Slavin, William J.
Summers, Raymond A.
Thompson, Herbert E.
Yeend, Robert N.

Seventy-two young men have been mustered in as members of Portage county's company to be incorporated into the 10th Regiment, Ohio National Guard. Of this number, sixty are Ravenna boys and thirteen are from Kent. In addition to the seventy-two who have passed their physical examination and been mustered into the service, the following young men have enlisted, but not yet been examined.

Ivan W. Shanafelt
William F. Meyers
Hubert C. Strayer
Cletus J. Weideman, Kent
Howard R. Bartholomew

Gerald E. Shanley
Frank W. Ferry
John Fisher
Thomas G. Gilson
George H. Smith

The lists are still open for seventeen more names and those desiring to join the colors may sign the enlistment roll at the Wonder Store where Mr. Neikirk has it in readiness.

It is announced that officers for the new Company will be appointed from its ranks by the War Department at Washington upon recommendation of the Colonel of Regiment. It seems to be the general opinion of the boys that Kingdon Siddall and Charles Cope will be appointed as commissioned officers. Siddall is now a member of Troop A., First Ohio Cavalry from which he will have to be honorably discharged should he enter the service of the Portage county company.

The boys who have been mustered in are now subject to the call of the War Department at Washington, which will be made at least ten days before the final order to go into mobilization camp, and in this connection, it is suggested that all of them who have jobs or positions remain where they are until the call shall come to leave them.

Sixty-five was the minimum number necessary to mustering in an organization of the home Company and that number will be increased to one hundred, the peace footing.

Up to Saturday evening, forty-five recruits had been examined and accepted and before Sunday evening the number had been increased to seventy-three. The people of Ravenna were given a thrilling surprise Saturday evening when these forty-five young citizen soldiers formed in military line and marched up Main Street, headed by the Ravenna city band and the Marine Italian band. Ringing addresses were made by Kingdon Siddall and W. J. Beckley and patriotism ran high through the community at the sight of the lads who had volunteered their services in defense of their country's rights and the national honor.

Enlistments began to come in much more rapidly after this demonstration and the list increased in rapid ratio until the sixty-five mark had been passed. It was a fine demonstration of instant loyalty to the flag and the boys are receiving merited praise.

On Sunday evening the members of the Company marched to the Methodist Episcopal Church in a body to attend the service arranged especially for them by the pastor, Rev. Charles H. Hauger. Long before the appointed hour, the church was filled to overflowing and it is estimated that three hundred people were unable to find admission.

The singing of national airs was the opening feature of the service and the music by orchestra and choir was a full expression of the hour. Anthems, soloists and quartets were selections appropriate.

To the Colors

This was the subject of an eloquent address by the pastor, Rev. C. H. Hauger, who made an earnest plea for all to stand by their country in this hour of crisis. "The issues," he said, "are now clear that this is not a war for revenge, or for territory or to repel the invader. Our president has stated this in words that will become in time as immortal as Lincoln's Gettysburg speech, we have entered this world conflict in the interests of humanity, for the sake of national and human rights. There is no turning back for a liberty-loving people. The war is on, but who shall go to this war? Shall young men be willing to stand on the sidewalk and cheer, until hoarse, other young men who count not their life dear to themselves, whose sisters and sweethearts choke back their emotion, brush away their tears and bravely smile with breaking heart? I leave you to answer whether the volunteer system is just. Congress has voted to put our money into this war, and now we must put our manhood and our womanhood alongside it. If we do not and are content to let others fight this great battle of democracy against autocracy, history will write of us like the shirking little town of Meroz in Palestine long ago. 'Curse ye America, curse ye bitterly the inhabitants thereof; because they come not to the help of the Lord against the mighty.'

"America's name will forever be the symbol of the 'shirker' and 'slacker' among the nations, and any citizen who refuses to heed the call for whatever service the country asks will help make it so, whether he be called to go to farm, factory or the front. Shame on the so-called citizen who is willing to see others fight the battles which settle great principles, having no part in the conflict, but sharing in the fruits of victory. He declared that too many are singing, 'We'll Dally Round the Flag, Boys,' which is why the world's ridiculing us by calling our government 'Uncle Sham.' There are too many blind optimists in the country who sit down and leave it all to God. But *GOD* helps those who help themselves, and a nation without deeds is a dead nation."

The clergyman paid touching tribute to the young men of the colors on whom he invoked Divine blessing and protection.

At the close of the service the pastor requested the volunteers to pass by the altar that he might shake their hands and bid them

God speed, and as they marched up the aisle to the singing of "Onward Christian Soldiers," the scene one of ineffacable memories.

Following honorable precedents, a movement is now on foot to raise a fund for use of the boys. The money will be placed with the proper official of the organization for occasions of emergency or special need for individual members of the company while in camps or other place of service.

Subscriptions to this fund will be received at the office at *The Republican.*

Major Love of Youngstown was here Saturday night in charge of the muster, assisted by Captain Christy, also of that city. The examining officer was First Lieutenant Earl Cliffe.

The Ravenna Republican:
Thursday, May 17, 1917
Soldier Boys to Attend Church
with Veterans of '61

Complete Roster of Portage County Company Which Will Attend Memorial Services with McIntosh Post and W.R.C. at Congregational Sunday Morning May 27.

Portage county's new military Company, one hundred strong, is awaiting orders to mobilize, but its members are still engaged at their various places of business and employment.

An invitation has been extended to the Company to attend the annual memorial service with the members of David McIntosh post, and the Women's Relief Corps at the Congregational church Sunday morning, May 27. The Relief Corps of the new company are requested to meet at G.A.R. Hall at ten A.M. where they will form in rank and march to the church.

The company will be photographed in a group following the church service.

The following is the muster roll of the Company complete:

1.	Anderson, Harold W.	Ravenna
2.	Anderson, Melvin G.	Ravenna
3.	Baldwin, Charles H.	Ravenna
4.	Bartholomew, H. R.	Ravenna
5.	Baxter, Clarence A.	Ravenna
6.	Blieu, Lewis C.	Ravenna
7.	Boak, Harold P.	Kent
8.	Boyd, Lawrence S.	Ravenna
9.	Brockett, N. A.	Freedom Station
10.	Brode, Arthur G.	Ravenna

11. Byers, John R.   Ravenna
12. Cannavino, Mark   Ravenna
13. Cannon, Clell C.   Kent
14. Carter, Joseph F.   Ravenna
15. Chambers, Floyd J.   Ravenna
16. Chickeno, Amelio   Ravenna
17. Clark, George   Ravenna
18. Conaway, Charles M. Ravenna
19. Cole, Joseph R.   Ravenna
20. Cope, Charles R.   Ravenna
21. Creque, Frank C.   Ravenna
22. Damicon, Leo A.   Ravenna
23. Davidson, George E. Ravenna
24. Davis, Claude M.   Kent
25. DeAngelis, Benjamin Ravenna
26. Dickens, Frederick   Ravenna
27. Diezman, Arthur L.   Ravenna
28. Dunning, Clair S.   Ravenna
29. Dustman, Dewey A.   Ravenna
30. Dyer, Edward F.   Ravenna
31. Elgin, Frank W.   Kent
32. Ferry, Frank W.   Kent
33. Fleishman, George P. Ravenna
34. Floyd, Otto S.   Ravenna
35. George, Kennerdell E. Kent
36. Gilson, Thomas G.   Raenna
37. Gless, Carl A.   Ravenna
38. Gray, William F.   Ravenna
39. Hallabaugh, Clifford F. Ravenna
40. Haas, Kennith M.   Ravenna
41. Hawk, Ralph E.   Kent
42. Horne, William F.   Ravenna
43. Hubbell, Harold L.   Ravenna
44. Jackson, Wallace N.   Ravenna
45. Jacobson, Berger H.   Ravenna
46. James, Nicholas   Ravenna
47. Jones, John H.   Kent

48. Jones, LeRoy   Ravenna
49. Keeter, Walter J.   Ravenna
50. Kick, Luther M.   Ravenna
51. Knapp, James F.   Ravenna
52. Krieble, Emerson P.   Ravenna
53. Lackey, John W.   Kent
54. Lauver, Roy B.   Ravenna
55. Lindsay, Robert J.   Ravenna
56. Long, Raymond E.   Ravenna
57. Lutz, William E.   Kent
58. Marsh, Jesse L.   Ravenna
59. Marsh, Shearold, L.   Ravenna
60. McKeever, George W.   Ravenna
61. Meyers, William F.   Kent
62. Miller, Maxwell M.   Kent
63. Minnich, Wilber C.   Ravenna
64. Moon, George H.   Kent
65. Moore, Walter O.   Ravenna
66. Mosier, Leon   Ravenna
67. Mott, Harold   Ravenna
68. Murphy, Dave N.   Ravenna
69. Myers, George W.   Kent
70. Parson, George W.   Ravenna
71. Price, Earl C.   Ravenna
72. Puffer, Harry S.   Ravenna
73. Renato, Joseph   Ravenna
74. Rice, Alva B.   Ravenna
75. Rock, John   Ravenna
76. Rufi, Joseph   Ravenna
77. Ruggiere, Tony   Ravenna
78. Sawyer, Bennet J.   Kent
79. Shanafelt, Ivan W.   Kent
80. Shanley, Gerold E.   Kent
81. Schultz, Joseph D.   Ravenna
82. Schultz, Elmer E.   Ravenna
83. Simpson, Walter A.   Kent
84. Skilton, William B.   Ravenna

85. Slavin, William J.   Ravenna
86. Smith, George H.   Ravenna
87. Smith, William, B.   Ravenna
88. Sprecht, Samuel C.   Ravenna
89. Strayer, Hubert G.   Kent
90. Swartout, Howard E.   Kent
91. Summers, Raymond A.   Ravenna
92. Thompson, Herbert E.   Ravenna
93. Trexler, William H.   Ravenna
94. Weideman, Cletus J.   Kent
95. Weldy, Hiram B., Jr.   Ravenna
96. Wilt, Harry D.   Kent
97. Yeend, Robert N.   Ravenna
98. A. E. Hoff, Sergeant, transferred from 2nd Missouri Infantry
99. Kingdon Siddall, transferred from Troop A., First Ohio Calvary.
100. John Stidsen, transferred from Co. F., 8th O.V.I.

Ravenna furnishes 74 of the 100; Kent, 22; Freedom, 1; Co. F., 1; and Missouri 2nd Infantry, 1.

The Ravenna Republican:
Thursday, May 24, 1917
Orders to Increase to Full War Strength

Portage County Company O. N. G. to Bring Total
Enlistments to 153 Men and Officers

Orders were received on Tuesday from Adjutant General Wood to recruit the Portage county regiment, unit of the 10th Ohio National Guard, to its full strength of one hundred and fifty-three men and officers. Recruiting headquarters have been reopened at the Ravenna town hall, in charge of First Lieutenant Charles R. Cope, who has been given until June 4 to complete the additional enlistments.

Kingdon Siddall, transferred from the Ohio Calvary, is Captain of the new Company, Charles R. Cope is First Lieutenant and Harold L. Hubbell is Second Lieutenant.

The 100 men already enrolled and sworn in and who constitute the peace footing of the organization, were drilled at the town hall, Wednesday evening by Captain Siddall.

Major Love of Youngstown has been promoted to the office of Lieutenant Colonel.

The Ravenna Republican:
Thursday, May 31, 1917
Throng of Citizens Join in Tribute to Soldier Dead

Largest Parade in Many Years—Ceremonies Doubly Impressive at This Time of the Nation's Crisis—Ringing Words from the Speaker of the Day—Company M., O.V.I. and Boy Scouts Join Veterans in Line of March

The observance of Decoration Day in Ravenna was one of large and impressive character in which nearly all of the citizens of the town participated either as spectators or in the line of march. Not for years has this community witnessed such a demonstration.

There was an especially large procession of school children, representing city and parochial schools, and nothing in the program was more inspiring or more thrilling than the sight of the bright-faced boys and girls.

There was the usual salute of cannon at the courthouse park in the afternoon followed by the assembling of those who were to participate in the parade. The line of march began on Main Street at Walnut Street and extended west to Chestnut, north to Highland Avenue, west to Sycamore, south to Main and east to the court house where disbandment was made.

The parade was headed by the Ravenna City Band, followed by civil war veterans, the W.R.C., Company M., 10th O.V.I., Red Cross Nurses in automobile; the Boy Scouts under the leadership of John Parham, and the longest line of schoolchildren ever seen in Ravenna.

The Boy Scouts attracted particular attention with the recruits of Company M and the cheering reached its climax when the Red Cross van appeared with its nurses and equipment.

The exercises were opened by the singing of "America" by the schoolchildren. This was followed with invocation by Rev. Francis

McIlwain, Rector of Grace Episcopal Church, after which the audience joined in the singing of "The Star Spangled Banner," led by the band, and the pupils of the lower grades recited Lincoln's Gettysburg Speech. The general order of General John A. Logan, issued May 5, 1868 was read by Major N. C. Lawrence, establishing Decoration Day. Major Lawrence spoke in warm praise of the boys who have enlisted to defend the flag in its new peril from the enemies of human liberty. He spoke of the armies of Washington and Lincoln, which were made up of volunteers and that the people of the great Republic could always be depended upon to defend the principles for which the nation's flag was unfurled.

Memorial Cross was decorated for the twenty-two soldiers sleeping in southern graves by members of David McIntosh Post, Grand Army of the Republic and by the Women's Relief Corps. After this solemn ceremony Major Lawrence introduced Rev. C. H. Hauger, pastor of the Ravenna Methodist Episcopal Church, who said in part:

> Three hundred thousand soldiers of the Union lie buried in seventy-nine national cemeteries. In some of these cemeteries, an army of over ten thousand unknown dead soldiers was consigned to rest while thousands were buried on lonely hillsides or in quiet valleys. The sacrifice of these unknown heroes was doubtly patriotic, worthy of highest eulogy. While their names are lost in oblivion, their deeds are immortal for they counted not the cost and sought not the applause of men or the eulogies of those who might sound their names in panegyrics. They were content just to do and die.

He reminded his listeners that every great cause for which men demand the service of a great army of obscure individuals citing the example of the unknown stokers in the *Titanic* disaster and the pages and bell boys who went to their cabins that others might be saved. They will never be forgotten nor will the heroes of the battlefield who have left memories more imperishable than those of any name. Men may forget names, but never the deeds of heroes.

Over fifty years have passed since the days of '61 and '65. Time may roll into centuries, but the struggle of those who perished that this nation might live will never be forgotten. And now that war has come again, we shall not fail to honor the men who fought for the preservation of the Union. All the more will we wend our way to national cemeteries and to the shrine of those who counted not their lives dear that liberty and democracy might live. Who will estimate the value of the sacrifice made by the soldiers of 1776, 1812, 1845, 1861, and 1898?

They saved and handed down the principle that all men are created free and equal, and it is ours to preserve and proclaim this to all the world.

This heritage is threatened today by one of the most militaristic powers in all history; a power that would enthrone might and brute force over right and human liberty; a power that is cruel and ruthless to the extreme of inhumanity in carrying out the purpose of worldwide rule, and would send us back to the jungle philosophy of the survival of the strongest in which love, mercy, compassion, pity and humanity have no part.

The speaker said that the supreme test of the nation has come. The preservation of civilization, the ultimate overthrow of militarism and of brute force are plainly the issues involved in the present world crisis. The triumph of democracy and freedom and the final overthrow of autocracy and oppression must be the final outcome if liberty and freedom are to live. Too costly has been the price paid for them to allow an autocratic power to wrest them from us.

The path of civilization is one of blood. Nothing has been gained that has not been wrested from our lowest nature by blood. As great armies have marched back and forth over the earth so has civilization advanced and retreated. The last great drive that shall deal a paralyzing blow to autocracy and bring the final peace and brotherhood to man is on.

Militarism has made the central powers mad. At the very start of the war they announced that they had thrown aside the book of rules written by civilization and adopted the policy of brute force in its stead. It has become plain that the only way to cope with such political insanity is to crush it by the force of superior armies, for you cannot reason with it or appeal to it in the name of humanity or honor which it neither heeds nor possesses. Ask Belgium, Germany's blood raw victim, if this is not true. Ask torn and bleeding France what the world may expect from the triumph of German arms and their barbarous tyranny.

War's Place in History

Much as we abhor war, we have to recognize the truth of history that civilization is born of strife and struggle. This republic was born by war and abolished slavery by war, and the republic of France, the pride of the world today in her honor and courage, came of the bloody spasm of revolution that overthrew her tyrants. Few people have become civilized by choice, and war will have a place in the world's program until the development of brain has overcome the destructive instincts of the race. Religion and education have many times had to ride in the wake of war and await its issue. Dreadful though it be, bloodshed and the discipline of war have generally prepared the way for civilization and spiritual progress, and it may well be that a nation drunk with militarism and the lust of power must be taught a similar lesson. The hour of God's clock has struck many times in history, and it has struck again in the rape of bleeding Belgium, in the ruthless slaughter of innocent women and children, the sinking of hospital ships and peaceable passenger boats. The civilized world has looked on until with stern indignation it has said thus far and no further shall this go on.

America's mission is clear in this crisis.

A War for Humanity

It is a war to save what she has already achieved and to prevent the world from slipping back into the prison house of tyranny. It is a war for posterity, a war that honors the memory of our soldiers death, a war for future peace. Who is there that will hesitate to what has been so honorably handed down and so heroically defended? Can we better honor our dead heroes than to dedicate ourselves anew to the flag for which they died? To falter would be a tragedy for the liberty-loving world has turned to America to save it from the destroyer, and our political salvation is at stake as well, for it has come to pass that "united we stand, divided we fall."

Benediction was pronounced by Rev. McIlwain. The customary decoration of soldier's graves was made in the morning by G.A.R. and W.R.C. committees.

The Ravenna Republican:
Monday, June 4, 1917
Enlistments Stop Tonight

At this writing, the names of twenty-five recruits of Company M., Ohio Infantry, have been added to the former list, leaving twenty-eight more to be obtained by enlistment. If these are not forthcoming by midnight of this day, the gap will be filled by draft, as no more enlistments will be taken after that hour. The recruits will be inspected by a federal officer this week, and the new volunteers will be subjected to physical examination at once. Beginning with today, the Company will use Riddle Hall No. 5 as its armory.

The following are the names of the latest volunteers: James N. LeRoy, Eugene Richardson, Gilbert C. John, Virgil Terrell, Carl R. Hentz, Charles R. Densmore, Henry S. Polglaze, Howard C. Sanders, Ben Piazzi, Forest C. Pemberton, Rollin F. Ditzman, Edward R. Palm, Ravenna; Lynn A. Davis, Charles C. Ballist, Fred A. Long, Ralph J. Weiss, Thomas Edward Jones, Frank Macherone, Mitchel Spangler, Harry C. Fisher, J. B. Clinger, Kent; Chester Keys, Atwater; Dennis Swartz, Suffield; Leon K. Gilbert, Barberton.

The Ravenna Republican:
Monday, July 5, 1917
Company M Goes into Camp at Macon, Georgia, July 15

Unofficial Word Only Awaits Confirmation from Headquarters. Recruiting Closes with 121 Enlistments First Consignment of Equipment Has Arrived—Boys Are Getting Ready to Leave

Company M, 10th Ohio Volunteers, is looking hourly for orders to go into camp at Macon, Georgia, July 15.

A portion of the equipment was received at headquarters, Tuesday, consisting in the main of ten pairs of trousers, 120 pairs of shoes, sixty-one pairs of leggings and other smaller items of outfit. The remainder of the equipment is expected this week. Each soldier will have a hat, two suits of underwear, pair of trousers, six pairs of hose, pair of shoes, shirt, blouse and will carry his rifle and one half of a bunk or shelter tent. The camp stove has also been received and pickaxes and shovels are on the road.

Recruiting closed on July 1 with a total of 121 enlisted and accepted volunteers who have been sworn into the service of the United States Army for the period of the war.

While nothing definite has been received concerning the date of departure for France, it is not believed that the boys will be transported across the water for another year. But they are ready for anything and are counting on nothing as a fixed certainty until official orders have been received. In the meantime, they are getting ready for duty by drill and preparation for the life of the camp.

The company is officered by Captain Kingdon T. Siddall, First Lieutenant, Charles R. Cope and Second Lieutenant, Harold L. Hubbell, all of Ravenna. The names of the enlisted men include those of

Harold W. Anderson, Melvin C. Anderson, Charles H. Baldwin, Howard R. Bartholomew, Charles H. Baxter, Lewis C. Blieu, Harold P. Boke, Lawrence R. Boyd, Norman H. Brockett, Arthur G. Brode, John R. Byers, Mark Cannavino, Clell C. Cannon, Joseph Carter, Floyd S. Chambers, Amelio Chickeno, George Clark, Charles M. Conaway, Joseph R. Cole, Frank C. Creque, Leo A. Damicon, George E. Davidson, Claude M. Davis, Jr., Ben DeAngelis, Frederick Dickens, Arthur L. Diezman, Clair S. Dunning, Dewey A. Dustman, Edward F. Dyer, Frank W. Elgin, Frank W. Ferny, Geo. P. Fleshman, Otto S. Floyd, Kennerdell E. George, Thomas G. Gilion, Carl A. Gless, Wm. F. Gray, Clifford L. Hollabaugh, Kenneth M. Hase, Ralph E. Hawk, Wm. E. Horne, Wallace N. Jackson, Berger H. Jacobus, Nick James, Edward J. Gilson, John H. Gilson, John H. Jones, Leroy Jones, Walter J. Keeter, Luther M. Kick, James F. Knapp, Emerson P. Krieble, John M. Lackey, Roy B. Lawver, Robert J. Lindsey, Raymond Long, Wm. B. Lutz, Jess L. Marsh, Shirl L. Marsh, Geo. M. McKeefer, Wm. Myers, Maxwell M. Miller, Wilbur C. Minnich, Geo. M. Moon, Walter J. Moore, Leon S. Mosier, Harold Mott, David N. Murphy, George W. Myers, Geo. W. Parsons, Earl C. Price, Harry S. Puffer, Joe Renato, Alva B. Rice, John Rock, Joe Rufi, Tony Rugieri, Bennett J. Sawyer, Irvin W. Shanafelt, Gerald E. Shanley, Elmer E. Schultz, Joseph D. Schultz, Walter A. Simpson, Wm. B. Skilton, Wm. J. Slavin, Geo. H. Smith, Wm. R. Smith, Samuel C. Specht, Herbert Strayer, Raymond A. Summers, Howard E. Swartout, Herbert E. Thompson, Wm. F. Trexler, Cletus J. Weidman, Hiram B. Weldy Jr., Harry Wilt, Robert N. Yeend, Cleon L. Parker, Charles V. Leroy, Harry C. Fisher, John C. Kennedy, Chas. H. Sanders, Carl R. Hentz, Raymond L. Hill, Chester Keys, Michael Spangler, Ezra K. Creese, Raleigh K. Merydith, Frank Valento, Dennis Swartz, Charles R. Byers, Jim Larcus, Thomas E. Jones, Ben Piazz, Gilbert A. John, John Klinger, Chas. R. Densmore, Lynn H. Dustin, Henry S. Polglase, Royce R. Hubbard, Frank Maccarone, Forest Pemberton.

The Ravenna Republican:
Monday, July 16, 1917
Company M Formally Mobilized and Now Is in Training

Awaiting Call to Go into Camp at Montgomery, Alabama Will Be among First Troops to See Service Abroad—Captain Siddall Receives Orders Sunday Afternoon

Company M, the new Portage county unit of the Tenth Ohio Infantry, was formally mobilized at Ravenna, Sunday at twelve o'clock, noon, pursuant to the call of President Wilson, and orders from the War Department received by Captain K. T. Siddall late Saturday night.

The men who responded to this call may well be regarded as the flower of the community and now stand as United States soldiers who have volunteered to serve their country during the present hostilities. They will be immediately subjected to the rigorous discipline of the army during a war period, and be among the first to see service abroad. All Ohio troops are named in the units first called by the president.

All men in Company M have given up their civil pursuits for a schedule of training in military conduct, drill and varied physical exercises. This preliminary training at Ravenna is calculated to harden and prepare the men to best endure the change in temperature and living conditions incident to their first week in Montgomery, Alabama, the camp designated for Ohio troops in the service of the United States.

It is believed that full equipment will be received some time during the week. About one half of the men are equipped with uniforms, with no field equipment except stoves and cooking utensils, which have recently arrived. Cots have been donated by Fairchild & Son and Manager D. G. Hartmen of Brady Lake. Men who do not live in Ravenna are quartered at the Riddle Hall No. 5. War Department contracts have been made with Mr. Hazen of the Etna House and Mr. Littrell of the North Chestnut Street restaurant to supply all enlisted men with meals.

The regulations of Company M require the presence of every man at Reveille roll call at seven-thirty each morning. A federal inspecting. officer is expected any minute, and military efficiency demands a Company be prepared for inspection without notice.

The men appear in enthusiastic spirits. The problem of selecting proper and efficient noncommissioned officers is a difficult and important task for the officers of the Company. Great emphasis is placed on personal hygiene of the men, and those who by conduct and example are the most likely to enforce sanitary rules will be given preference for these positions, provided they display the spirit that will get things done in the shortest possible time. The following have received warrants as Sergeants and have been assigned to duty by Captain Siddall: Robert N. Yeend, First Sergeant; Harold W. Anderson, Supply Sergeant; Joseph Carter, Line Sergeant, and Elmer (Bill) Cook is assigned as Company Clerk. Sergeant Hoff of Missouri have joined and both officers and men are elated over the enlistment of Bill Conway as cook. Conway has showed ability in the field and in Ravenna hotels. He says Company M has the best bunch of boys he has "looked over."

The total strength of the Company consists of three officers, 122 enlisted men and eight applicants awaiting physical examinations. This report was made to General Barry at Chicago Sunday afternoon.

In response to the solicitation for funds made by the *Republican*, a total of $274 has been turned over to the Company for the benefit of the boys, who will need many things not provided for them by the government.

Every man is equipped with a complete comfort kit, the handiwork of members of the Old Northwest Chapter, D.A.R. and the Ravenna Red Cross. The story is also out that Mr. John Watters of East Main Street has a surprise package for every man in the company, and anyone acquainted with Mr. Watters will believe the story to be well-founded.

The ladies of the W.R.C. have invited the entire Company to a banquet to be served tonight at the Church of Christ.

In case the Company is still in Ravenna next Sunday, a patriotic service will be held in its honor at the Congregational Church at an hour to be announced later.

The *Republican* takes this occasion to endorse every man in Company M and to exhort this community to a manifestation of its just pride in the contribution it is about to make to the cause of humanity when it marches away and begins a journey that has no fixed course and no definite end, obeying orders and following the flag and the path of honor.

The Ravenna Republican:
Monday, August 20, 1917
Company M Ready for Camp or War Across the Seas

Boys in Fine Health and Spirits, with Hard Daily Training to Prepare Them for Arduous Work—Has First Rating Among Ohio Volunteer Troops

During the week Captain Siddall received orders from Washington to send fifteen members of the Company to Camp Perry on Lake Erie, near Sandusky, much to the regret of the boys, who had planned on being together during their service. On Friday noon nearly the whole town escorted them to the Baltimore and Ohio depot, headed by the Ravenna band where they were taken to Cleveland on a special troop train. Those transferred are: James Adair, George Clark, Lawrence Boyd, Frederick Dickens, Gilbert John, Luther Kick, James Larcus, Leon Mosier, Harry Puffer, Ravenna; Frank Ferry, Raleigh Meredith, Bennett Sawyer, Michael Spangler, Ralph Hawk, Kent; Cletus Weideman, Suffield. The boys are ready for camp or for war across the seas. They are expecting the call to leave for camp at Montgomery, Ala., at any time and are getting ready. The fifteen thus transferred are to become a part of the 4th Ohio which lacks a full war quota. This regiment to be known as the 166th United States Infantry, is composed of picked troops from twenty-six states and is a part of the 42nd division of the U.S. Army known as the Rainbow division in command of Gen. W. A. Mann.

Ravenna Republican:
Monday, September 17, 1917
Ravenna Boys Write from Camp Sheridan, Montgomery

Weather of Healthy Hot Variety—Plenty of Hard Work. People Kind and Hospitable, but Charge Soldiers Big Prices. Boys Move Building by Carrying It

Writing from Camp Sheridan at Montgomery, Alabama, Freeman Mahan, son of Mr. and Mrs. W. H. Mahan of this city, details many interesting things which *The Republican* is permitted to present to its readers through the courtesy of Mrs. Mahan. Under date of August 27 he says in part:

> We are not settled yet by any means, but we have our cots and suitcases now. We all have mosquito nets to fasten over our cots and aside from that we are sleeping under the stars.
>
> There is not such a vast difference between the climate here and at home. The nights are quite cool and it is good and warm in the daytime—just the right combination to make one lazy.
>
> Our trip down was very interesting. As soon as we crossed the Ohio river from Indiana into Louisville, Kentucky, we could see the difference between the north and the south. Through Kentucky and Tennessee the houses were nearly all one story shacks with narrow one-inch boards tacked over the cracks to shut out the air, the entire building being whitewashed on the outside. The interior would make about two medium-sized rooms for a northern household of average numbers, and the families occupying these houses in Dixie land are nearly all large. Whites and blacks live in the same kind of houses in nearly all instances and we often passed places where they were living together.
>
> Our feed has been good enough but so small in quantity that it wouldn't feed a setting hen. The people seem to know this, so they drive into camp with bake stuff and vegetables which they sell.

I have seen fields of cotton, tobacco, sugar cane, sweet potatoes and broom corn, and we cut down a fig tree right in front of our mess hall yesterday.

We use horses in camp. We just have a long rope attached to a drag and a big bunch of us have to pull it. About five of the officers stand on the drag, so you imagine how near to real work it is.

In a letter dated August 30, his brother, Hugh Mahan, of Co. E, 1st Ohio Engineers, tells of work which tried their muscles and their endurance in preparing camp. He says they had to clean whole cotton fields and drag and harrow them to get them in readiness for the camp, and he had been in the woods all day cutting wood for cooking. They had to carry the wood for about one half mile. At that time their tents had not arrived, although they were expecting them soon. In the meantime they had been sleeping in the open. He describes the soil in that part of the country as red sand, with cotton and watermelons its products. They expected to go to town the next night to attend a reception to be given them by the Alabama troops.

Another letter from Freeman Mahan, written August 31, told of troop inspection and signing the pay roll that day creating a general cessation from work. He spoke of real southern weather, the excessively hot kind; "hot as the dickens," as he expressed it. They had mosquito nets to fasten over their cots, making it comfortable.

He spoke of the reception given them on the preceding night by the Montgomery people, which was followed by a dance. When some young fellows from town started to join in the program they were told that the dancing was restricted to soldiers.

"They are going to give a dance for us every week and they told the civilians that if they wished to dance they would have to get uniforms," he said.

The thing that touched him most was the sight of some of the old confederate soldiers who marched down the aisle of the hall carrying the American flag and wearing their gray uniforms.

It seemed to him that any fellow with warm blood in his veins could not stay out of the army after that. "I have begun to think that the south is more anxious than the north to forget the civil war," he said.

Speaking of the hospitality of the people, he says they are the most hospitable folks he ever saw. He told of an instance illustrating the good spirit of the citizens. He said that on the preceding night he waited for a comrade from Kent, Ohio, with whom he planned to go to town, thereby missing the truck that carried the rest of the boys. They started for the street car when they met a citizen who promptly told them to get into his wagon and took them to town, telling them that it was a pleasure to help the boys and that he would do so at every opportunity.

Speaking of their meals, he said they were getting pretty good grub, either that or they were getting used to it. He heard the cook say they would get meat only twice a week from that time on as it was too hot there to eat much of it. "Maybe that is the object of our coming here," he said, "to cut down on expenses." We line up for meals about twenty yards from the mess hall and when the whistle blows you ought to see the scramble. The fellows are all afraid that they will not get their share, as the last ones get a scanty meal. The tables are marked off at intervals to seat ten men and the food is placed on these spaces to feed just that number. Sometimes there is an abundance and again there is but a scant supply. Needless to say, I have always been "Johnny on the spot," and I am going to try mighty hard to keep it up.

Their tents had arrived and, "Gee, but we do sleep!" The most bothersome thing they have to endure is the little gnat of which there seems to be a billion to the square inch. They get in eyes, ears, nose and mouth and all over the men. He said he had not noticed the mosquitoes very much, but that some of the fellows complained about them, especially when they had to work in the woods.

The country there is chock full of turkey buzzards which are protected by the government because of their sanitary value. They are the scurviest looking birds he ever saw.

He told of a prospective barbecue to be provided for them by an old-time colored, with potatoes and salad and "fixins," all for a dollar a plate. "I am of the opinion he will find that we can eat our money's worth," he said.

Referring to the heat of the hour, he said the sweat was dropping from his chin at that moment and standing on his arms in great drops.

That while it was very warm, it was not a distressing heat, but the kind that makes one perspire and feel good for it.

He told of escaping a hard job that day by being on guard duty. There was a large building to be moved and instead of using horses or other ordinary methods they employed manpower after a fashion of the pyramid building days of ancient Egypt. Handles were fastened to the building and about two hundred soldiers got hold of them and literally carried it for about the distance of a square. "But my turn is likely to come tomorrow," he said.

The Mahan brothers and Charles Batsch enlisted at Cleveland with the Engineering Corps. Two Hudson youths, cousins, are also with them at Montgomery.

The Ravenna Republican:
Monday, September 17, 1917
Company Leaves Ravenna for Camp
Sheridan, Alabama

Depart for Montgomery, Sunday Morning, from Uptown Pennsylvania Depot—Citizens Accompany Them to Their Train En Masse and Give Them Goodbye and Godspeed

A picture of Company M, 10th Ohio Infantry, Portage county's volunteer youth who answered their country's call immediately following the declaration of war with Germany, was taken and included in the picture was Sergeant Joseph Carter, Sergeant Arthur E. Hoff, Captain Kingdon T. Siddall, Second Lieutenant Harold L. Hubbell, First Lieutenant Charles R. Cope, Frank Elgin, Howard Bartholomew, Amelio Chickeno, Mark Cannivino, Geo. Fleishman, Co., Bugler; Geo. Myers, Co. Bugler; Frank Maccherone, Jas. Adio, Joe Renato, Jas. Reale, Carl Elgin, William Conway, Co. Cook; Thomas Bosworth, John Rock, Frank Ferry, George Moon, Wilbur Minnich, Ivan Shanafelt, John Reigle, Michael Spangler, Clair S. Dunning, Raleigh Meredith, Sam Jewels, James Larcus, Harry Fisher, Ben DeAngles, George Davidson, Frank Valento, William Trexler, Joe Schultz, Ben Piazz, Frank Moff, Joe Rufi, Dennis Swartz, Herbert Strayer, Joseph Cole, Tony Ruggerie, William Slaven, Ben Sawyer, Willis E. Lutz, Harry Puffer, Ray Lawver, Chester Keys, Frederick Dickens, Thomas E. Jones, Melvin C. Anderson, Raymond Hentz, Raymond Long, Cletus Weideman, Harold Boak, Earl Wright, Ralph E. Hawk, Gilbert A. John, John H. Jones, Sergeant Elmer Schultz, Norman Brockett, Kennerdell George, Charles Byers, Walter Moore, William Skilton, Robert Kelley, Berger Jacobson, David Murphy, Shirl Marsh, Leon Mosier, Gerald E. Shanley, Forest Pemberton, Harold Mott, Clell Cannon, Clarence Baxter, John Byers, Sergeant Robert K. Yeend, Carl Gless, William Myers,

Charles Leroy, William Smith, Ezra Creese, Emerson Krieble, Nick James, Floyd Chambers, Lynn Dustin, Arthur Brode, Earl Price, Carl Vitzthum, Edward Dyer, Howard E. Swartout, Lawrence Boyd, Harold Baugh, Sergeant Walter A. Thompson, Sergeant Harold Anderson, Clifford Holabaugh, Luther M. Kick, Stanley Polglaze, Charles Sanders, Sam Lafalce, Christopher Spade, Clyde Reed, Raymond Summers, Herbert Nelle, Arthur Diezman, George Smith, George McKeever, Raymond Hill, Lewis Blieu, William Horne, Walter Horne, Walter Keeter, Herbert Thompson, Jesse Marsh, Hiram Bayne Weldy, Jr., Maxwell Miller, Frank Creque, Dewey Dustman, William Gray, James Knapp, Henry Baldwin, Cleon Parker, Otto Floyd, Clasto McReed, Alva B. Rice, Leroy Jones, William Jackson, Harold Haas, Kennett Haas, Lester Roller, John C. Kennedy, George Parsons, Harry Wilt, Edward Gilson, and Leo Damicon.

The Company is in command of Captain Kingdon T. Siddall, only son of Judge I. T. Siddall of this city. Captain Siddall was practicing law in Cleveland at the time of the threatened rupture between Mexico and the United States when he immediately enlisted as a member of Troop A, First Ohio Calvary, for service on the Mexican border where he remained for several months before the outbreak of the present war. At the organization of Company M he was transferred to Ravenna as its Captain. He was the unanimous choice of the Company. He is a graduate of Kenyon and Harvard Law School and sacrificed the beginning of a brilliant career to serve his country.

First Lieutenant Charles R. Cope and Second Lieutenant Harold L. Hubbell are also Ravenna boys. Cope was gunner in the Spanish American War and was awarded a first-class gunner's medal for his proficiency. Lieutenant Hubbell never saw military service but responded quickly.

Company M has gone and is somewhere on the road between Ravenna and Camp Sheridan at Montgomery, Alabama. The departure was made about seven o'clock Sunday morning in three special cars provided for the soldiers and a baggage car for their arms and impediments, including upwards of 138 lunch boxes provided by loving hands.

Captain Kingdon T. Siddall received word from regimental headquarters Thursday night for the Company to be in readiness to entrain within one hour and the work of getting ready for the final order for departure was commenced that night. Everything was packed, numbered and arranged for quick handling and during Friday most of the things were taken to the uptown Pennsylvania freight depot between Main street and Highland Avenue. The final order came in the early afternoon on Saturday to be ready to leave at five o'clock Sunday morning.

Arrangements were made for the ringing of the courthouse bell at four o'clock Sunday morning and in response to its summons citizens left their homes en masse and within a quarter of an hour a throng of people had assembled in front of the company headquarters in Riddle Hall No. 5 and soon the morning reveille sounded for the boys to arise and get themselves in readiness to leave their home barracks for the last time. In the meantime, the crowd rapidly increased by accessions from Kent, Atwater and other townships until Main Street was a mass of humanity between the barracks and the Pennsylvania crossing. It did not take the boys long to get themselves in readiness and soon the sound of the bugle was heard again, summoning them into line which was quickly formed on Prospect Street, the roll called and the final "Forward March!" given. It was a thrilling moment as the soldier youth took the first step in the march that was to take them from home, friends, and loved ones to camp and its preparatory work for the battlefront. There was no cheering or loud demonstration.

The cars had been on the siding since the preceding night and on arrival at the depot, the same expedition characterized the final acts of loading arms and other impediments in the baggage car and in the entraining of the soldiers. It was a triumphal procession and the fine spirit of heroism manifested by the young volunteers was something to remember and be proud of.

There was an interval of fully one hour between arrival and departure, thus giving the boys ample time to say their good-byes to mothers, sweethearts and other loved ones.

It seemed but a short time when the sound of the approaching locomotive was heard and in a few minutes the couplings were all made, the final good-byes said and amid waving of handkerchiefs and small flags the train began the journey that was to end at Montgomery.

The train went from here to Alliance. From that point it was transferred to the Ft. Wayne division of the Pennsylvania lines to Orrville, where it was again transferred to the C.A.&C., being closely followed by two other sections made up of troops from Youngstown, Salem, Alliance and Canton, arriving at Cincinnati Sunday evening.

Since the picture before departure was taken five members have been added to the company, being transferred from Alliance, as follows: Leon Hill, John Bernard, Thomas Bosworth, Peter Roller and Howard Baugh. Fifteen of the boys have been transferred to the Rainbow Division and at last word from them were at Mauntauk, Long Island, awaiting transport to France.

Sergeant Robert Yeend was unable to accompany the boys, being stricken with inflammatory rheumatism two weeks ago and is now bedfast at the home of his parents, Mr. and Mrs. J. C. Yeend.

The Ravenna Republican:
Thursday, September 20, 1917
With Company M on Its Trip to the South

The Republican's Special Representative Tells of Incidents Which Happened and of Impressions Recorded Along the Way. Company Appreciative of Favors Shown

Charles M. Conaway

(*The Republican* takes great pleasure in announcing that through arrangements made with Captain Kingdon Siddall, we will have an exclusive representative with Company M who will keep our readers in close touch with all the activities of the Company wherever the boys may be stationed. The services of Private Chas. M. Conaway have been secured and as he is a former member of *The Republican* staff and has had considerable other newspaper experience. His articles may well be looked forward to with anticipation.)

Monday afternoon finds the troop train, of which Company M makes up a section, making way leisurely south from Nashville, Tennessee, toward Montgomery, Alabama, on the tracks of the Louisville and Nashville railway.

Our train is made up of units from Salem, Canton, Massillon, and Ravenna, and we have with us Colonel C. C. Weybrecht of Alliance, where we picked up the Salem Company and the staff officers. From Alliance we went to Orrville over the Ft. Wayne by way of Canton and Massillon. The run from Orville to Columbus was over the C.A.&C. A short layover at Xenia was enlivened by musician George Myers and his band.This same organization gave impromptu concerts in all towns of any size during the first day out and have no small amount of credit due for all their efforts toward enlivening the trip.

Cincinnati was reached about six o'clock Sunday evening and we set out for Louisville, Kentucky about an hour later. The stop at Cincinnati will be remembered from the circumstance that Captain Siddall endeavored to release us from our cars for a short period of physical exercise, and, when some distance from the train, the order to move was given, a wild scramble ensuing in which several became separated from the bunch but all were eventually accounted for. Several were held up by the presence of Lieutenant Hubbell on the steps of a moving car, but willing hands cleared the way.

At Louisville, where we arrived at four-thirty Monday morning, we were ordered to detrain and take our places in the tourist cars provided at the station.

The new cars had been made ready for our reception and we were ordered to turn into the waiting berths and sleep until nine o'clock. An order obeyed with alacrity. Our cup of joy was filled when we were given a satisfying breakfast, piping hot from the mess, at a point between Louisville and Nashville.

Colonel Weybrecht ordered the entire battalion from the train at Nashville, under command of Major Cristy, and a combination review and legstretch was enjoyed, the command marching several blocks through the streets of that city.

Agricultural conditions and crops appear to be flourishing, as observed from our train. The boys are having strange crops pointed out to them as we go along. Among these are the large fields of tobacco, patches of sugarcane and cotton, and even brown sage. In the blue grass of Kentucky were seen many herds of fine cattle and some swine sighted are being certified as razorbacks of the first order.

A spot of historical interest, in that it recalled the great civil war, was a military cemetery we passed a few miles north of Nashville. Orderly rows of stone markers and well-kept greens gave it the appearance of a place held in greatest reverence and esteem. The fact that men from the northern states are being trained in the south for service abroad gives abundant proof of our unity and shows the old enmity has been wiped out.

Other Members of Company M

Robert Lindsay, son of Mr. and Mrs. E. C. Lindsay, of this city, is a member of Co. M and was in the ranks when the boys left for Camp Sheridan, Montgomery, Alabama, last Sunday morning (the 16th).

The Ravenna Republican:
Thursday, September 17, 1917
Company M Now Unit of 136th
Machine Gun Battalion

Equipment Is That of Rapid-Fire Guns and Considerable Portion of Unit Will Be Mounted—Early Departure from Montgomery Possible—Last of Ravenna Rations Used Up—Cook Conway Busy

By Charles M. Conaway

Sept. 20, 1917

The end of the third day of our stay at Camp Sheridan finds us comfortably settled under canvas and buckling down to the routine of real army life. Our days have been occupied with work incident to settling into our quarters, with only a half day of actual drill. Tents for the company officers have been erected, the company street improved, the mess hall ready for work and much other necessary labor has been performed. Another day of this will complete all to be done.

The Company street is partially completed and when finished will be a thing of picturesque beauty. A section runs through a slight ravine, shaded by beeches and pines, and this is to be made into a small park. Bridges have been built over the canal, which runs through it, underbrush has been cleared out, stumps cut away, and attractive benches will make it complete. Naturally, we share in the conveniences given the other units: a sewage system, electric lights, running water, by means of which shower baths are afforded, proper equipment for garbage disposal and others not common to the American soldiery of other generations.

The company mess, in charge of Sergeant Frank Elgin, is improving day by day. We take our meals in a well-arranged wood mess hall, nicely screened in, and the work and time of serving the men is lessening. Cook William Conway takes pride in his kitchen and his work meets with the approval of all visiting officers, and sanitary conditions are in accordance with the rules of the sanitation department inspectors. The last of the rations procured in Ravenna are being used up and arrangements have been made with the commissary department for an issue of government rations. These will include fresh meat, regulation bread, etc.

The commissioned officers of the company are taking their meals at the mess hall for now but will transfer shortly to the regular officer's mess. An offer to cook for this has been extended to Cook William Conway. The quality and quantity of food furnished is carefully watched by Captain Siddall, and Lieutenants Cope and Hubbell.

Access to the showers is permitted the men at all times and are a source of real pleasure. Proper bathing in a camp is more than that in this hot, dry climate where everything is sand coated and dust-covered. For the present the showers are utilized as a company laundry and the boys certainly turn out efficient work for amateurs in this line. Laundering is done by a number of Montgomery cleaning companies and by numerous colored women.

Postal facilities are being improved and both outgoing and incoming mail are taken care of properly, either through the regimental chaplain or the YMCA.

Mail addressed to any person in Company M. 10th Ohio If., Camp Sheridan, Montgomery, Alabama is sure of reaching its destination.

The work of the YMCA is an important factor in the camp. The various headquarters are places of recreation, music, helpful lectures and writing conveniences are furnished, and are nightly filled with groups of young men.

The company band manages to find time to practice with their new equipment and promise to develop into a first-class organization. New music, popular selections mostly, is to be furnished by a Montgomery dealer and real concerts will be in order. Musicians from other tent infantry companies have been secured, including a bass, three cornets, three trombone players, and one drummer. An offer has been made to Musician Myers, who is in charge of the band, to give a concert in Montgomery. Acceptance will be made later, depending upon the alacrity with which the members take up the work and their ability to work together.

Wednesday afternoon and evening was visiting day in the city. Several improved the opportunity and came back with various impressions of the populace. All agreed that everything they had heard concerning southern friendliness was true. Many purchases were made, all intended to contribute to the comforts of the camp.

A trolley runs near the camp proper and access to the city is comparatively easy.

Captain Siddall's announcement that our company has been changed into a machine gun organization was greeted with much enthusiasm by all, Wednesday noon at mess. Company M will be one of three units of similar size from the 10th to be transferred and will be under the command of our present battalion commander, Major John A. Logan, of Youngstown, O. Companies J, K, and L are the other units and the whole will be known as the 136th Machine Gun Battalion. Our equipment will be rapid fire guns, and a considerable part of the unit will be mounted. An early departure from Camp Sheridan is a possibility, due to the necessity for a small arms firing range of sufficient capacity for our machine guns.

Army canteens are in operation in the various regimental camps and almost every necessity and many luxuries are offered for sale.

Lieutenant Rew, U.S.R., a Fort Benjamin Harrison man, has been attached to the company for the present, ranking next to Lieutenant Hubbell. Lieutenant Rew is a practical, proficient officer.

Work on regimental headquarters is progressing and comfortable, pleasant quarters for Colonel C. C. Weybrecht and his staff, as well as battalion and company officers, have been provided.

A welcome issue of mosquito nets, ponchos, etc., has come to us through the quartermaster's department, by way of Sergeant Anderson. Much needed clothing is promised for the near future.

Several visitors from Ravenna and Kent boys in other units have been with us at odd moments and some of our fellows have been busy looking up friends from back home.

The impressive ceremony of guard mount attracts and holds the interest of practically all during the time the formation is in progress.

A quartet is being formed under the auspices of of Private Ezra Creese.

The Ravenna Republican:
Monday, October 1, 1917
Company M Becomes Company C 136th
Machine Gun Battalion

Rumors of Desertions without Foundation—Heavy Rainstorm Does Considerable Damage—Captain Siddall May Go to France

By Charles M.Conaway

Camp Sheridan, Sept. 24, 1917

An undercurrent of rumor has reached the Ravenna boys here that several of their number deserted the service during the trip south and are being sought by federal officials. Captain K. T. Siddall, commanding officer of the Ravenna contingent, desires to discredit these stories as being without foundation and to say that he reached Camp Sheridan with each and every man whose name appears upon the muster roll of the company, excepting Sergeant Robert Yeend, detained at home by illness.

In this connection, it can be said that Captain Siddall has received applications from twelve men, members of other companies, to enter Company C. and Private Ralph Snell, Company A. 10th Infantry, has been accepted.

Private Snell is a brother of Sergeant Snell, Sergeant Major, 136th Machine Gun Battalion. This desire on the part of others to be enrolled with us speaks well of our good standing and fellowship.

A word of explanation is in order as regards the transfer of Company M. 10th Infantry, into the 136th Machine Gun Battalion and is known as Company C of that organization. Captain Siddall ranked as the third captain in the Tenth and becomes the second ranking captain of this new arm of the service. According to the new system of organization, each company in the battalion will be officered by a captain, five Lieutenants and fourteen sergeants and fourteen corporals. The sergeants include ten line sergeants and four special sergeants, first, supply, mess and stable. The roster of the company also includes forty-five first class privates, one horseshoer, one saddler and eighty-nine privates, a total of 177 men.

The company commanded by the junior captain of each battalion has been disbanded and the strength of the remaining units will be increased by the reassignments of the officers and men.

A heavy rainstorm visited this section Sunday night and Monday, making it necessary to repair much of the ditching around the camp site. The entire company turned out and details, working under Lieutenant Cope and Hubbell, rebuilt the bridge spanning the drain ditch which crosses the company street, and remade the street.

The overflow caused by the bridge on the company street, flooded the tents of the sergeants and caused both discomfort and inconvenience. They saved much of their property only by quick work. The march to the mess hall for breakfast was through mud thrown up by the overflow and under the cover of the recently issued ponchos.

The company street is worked up in nice shape and is a tribute to the engineering skill of Lieutenant Hubbell. Lieutenant Cope and his picked force of pick and shovel experts who tore out the old bridge and built a new one in record time.

Work on the street was lessened by the use of a road machine, loaned by a neighboring planter to Captain Siddall for use in making a regimental parade ground, drawn by a span of our mules belonging to the supply department. The assistance of the two brothers, Shirl and Jesse Marsh, was invaluable in handling the scraper and managing the mules. Corporal Hubbard also gave expert assistance with the mule teams. The verdict of the company in general was that the Marsh boys must be working out their taxes on the road and using some of the knowledge and experience gained on the Portage county roads.

Music with our meals! Captain Siddall has purchased a phonograph of convenient size for use in the mess hall and will supply a variety of records, including the latest popular selections.

It is rumored about the camp that Captain Siddall, of Company C., 136th Machine Gun Battalion, will be one of several officers sent abroad for special training in the use of machine guns and for observation of machine fire. The period of training, as outlined by the Montgomery papers, covers six weeks, after which the officers will return to their respective commands. Young men and men of extensive schooling are to be chosen, says the report, and Captain Siddall certainly possesses the necessary qualifications.

When interviewed, Captain Siddall seemed reticent to discuss the subject but insisted that he would remain with his company.

Musician George Myer's band is being strengthened by several musicians from other units of our battalion and will act in the capacity of a band to the battalion.

Mail intended for members of the company should be addressed to Company C., 136th Machine Gun Battalion, Camp Sheridan, Montgomery, Alabama.

The Ravenna Republican:
Thursday, October 4, 1917
Terrific Hurricane Strikes Camp Sheridan

Sergeant Yeend Arrives—Reorganization of Company Brings Promotions—Change of Camp Site Held Up—Transfers to Headquarters Company

By Charles M. Conaway

Sept. 29, 1917

While *The Republican* representative at the Ohio camp is writing this, we are emerging from a tropical storm of hurricane proportions, which has held this section in its grip for the past three days. The storm had its beginning Thursday morning and held on until late Saturday. All military activities have been suspended and only such work as has been made necessary by the excess of moisture has been performed.

A heavy downpouring of rain and a high wind, reported as being a seventy-four mile an hour velocity by the *Montgomery Journal,* marked the advent of the storm proper, breaking upon us and continuing unabated until 4:30 Saturday morning. The direction of the gale was toward the southwest and touched here as it turned toward the gulf again after an easterly course.

Although the location of Company C camp is not an especially sheltered one, no material damage was done with the exception of the flooding of one tent occupied by some of the sergeants and the first sergeant's tent was washed down. Much of the inconvenience of this was lessened by the fact that the occupants had moved into the mess hall. This state of affairs is due to their location in a wide ravine. The tentage of the company stood up well during the wind and rain and not a single one was blown down and only a few leaked.

The company street is a mass of mud and moving about is difficult. A section of the street was damaged by the overflow making repairs necessary.

An incident in connection with the coming of the hurricane was an alarm sent out Wednesday night and spreading throughout the entire three battalions, that a storm similar to a typhoon was bearing down upon this city, and vicinity at a speed in excess of 150 miles an hour. Immediately an order came up line for everyone to turn out and dress and be ready to combat the gale. At once the sound of stake pounding, rope tightening and other precautionary measures was heard in all directions; many not even waiting to array themselves in full attire. The excitement ran so high that even Lieutenant Cope and Corporal Byers bestowed themselves to make ready for the emergency by staking down their racing car. Fifteen minutes later quiet and order was resumed, due to activities of certain sergeants in quieting the rumor, and not a few set out to look for the perpetrator of the hoax. Our one solace during this period of mud and rain has been that our meals have been served regularly and that no one leaves the mess hall hungry.

First Sergeant Robert Yeend arrived in camp Friday noon and been kept busy acquainting himself with our progress.

Captain Siddall has arranged that each man contribute a small sum monthly from his pay to a common fund for the benefit of Cook William Conway. This plan has been formulated to insure that the cook receive compensation commensurate with his ability and the company shows its approval of his work. Visitors from other units testify that Company C enjoys the best mess in the entire camp.

The reorganization of the Company has made opportunity for the promotion of four corporals to sergeants and three privates to the rank of corporals. Corporals Harold Haas, Royce Hubbard, Joseph Schultz and Carl Hentz were made sergeants and Privates Long, Keyes and George were made corporals.

The change from our present campsite to the new one has been held up by the inclement weather. Special permission from headquarters has been secured for a new arrangement of the tents.

Captain K. T. Siddall disposed of his first case since his appointment to the position of summary court officer this morning. The offender, a non-commissioned officer of old Company C, 10th Ohio, was demoted and discharged from custody. Thirteen other prisoners await trial for various offenses, none of them having any connection with our company.

A total of forty-three men have been transferred from other units to this company. We received twenty-eight from old Company I, 10th Infantry, and fifteen from Company B, 136 M. G. Battalion, the former coming from Coshocton and the latter from Canton.

Monthly muster will be held tomorrow (Sunday) afternoon and another pay day will be due in a few days. On account of the fact that the disbursing quartermaster is located here, more regular pays may be expected. Regulars transferred to the headquarters company have been arranged, including teamsters and clerks. None of those transferred will be far removed from this company.

The Ravenna Republican:
Thursday, October 11, 1917
News from Company C 136th
Machine Gun Battalion

Members Visit Capitol Building—Sights on Fifteen Mile Hike, Machine Gun Range Located Twenty Miles from Camp Sheridan

By Charles M. Conaway

October 6, 1917

The close of our third week at Camp Sheridan is marked by almost perfect weather. The days are warm and bright, but the advent of the cooler days of autumn can be noticed.

Saturday and Sunday are the days allowed the soldiers for their own and practically all took advantage of the respite from drill, to plan and carry out various excursions and programs of amusement. After the Saturday morning inspection conducted for C Company by Captain William McCord, Company B, 136th Machine Gun Battalion, and his lieutenants, the men busied themselves by putting their effects in order in the various tents. Following this, a movement in all directions was noticeable, all going for a visit with friends in other outfits until the noon mess call.

In the afternoon the company wilted away by twos and threes, all clad in clean, nicely pressed clothes and wearing the regulation broad black tie. The Auburn college—Company C, 146th Infantry (8th Ohio) football game drew a considerable Ravenna attendance. Others set out shopping while several went on excursions to the banks of the Alabama River.

The Alabama Capitol

The Republican representative, in company with Thomas Jones and Clair Dunning, visited the capitol building Saturday afternoon. The structure is of marble, and in design resembles the national capitol at Washington. It is located upon one of the highest points in the city and commands a spendid view in all directions.

The floors are of wood and marble and the furnishings of mahogany. The wooden stairs are well-worn and imagination easily peoples them with the historic characters of former days.

The principal places of interest to the *Ravenna* visitors were the historical museum and the balcony of the rotunda, commanding a view of the city.

A splendid collection of stoneware, pottery, flints, arrow heads and the like tell of early Indian history. An iron cannon, about a three pounder, marks the time of Bienville's attempts at settling Mobile.

The Civil War collection was gathered under the auspices of the Sophie Bibb chapter of the Daughters of the Confederacy.

The hall occupied by the historical museum is the one in which the Secession ordinance was passed on January 11, 1861.

A timely tip to the colored custodian enabled us to view the city from the rotunda balcony. After climbing several flights of winding stairs, we stood under the flag of the state of Alabama and looked out over the city. To the west spread out the business section and the Alabama river, to the south west the residential district and in the distance on the north, the Ohio camp, the brown tents and wooden mess halls being plainly visible at a distance of four miles.

Leaving the building, we stood over the spot where Jefferson Davis took the oath as President of the Confederate States of America, February 18, 1861.

A Fifteen Mile Hike

Captain Siddall treated his command to a "hike" of considerable proportions Friday forenoon, in place of the regular schedule of drill.

We set out at seven-forty AM and followed a westerly direction out of the reservation and into a well-graveled turnpike. After leaving the limits of the camp, "route order" was given and we visited with one another while we swung along the road. The trip consumed three hours and thirty-five minutes and three halts were made.

Much of special interest was noted, including the new base hospital, intended to accommodate the cases of serious illness developing among 40,000 soldiers to be located here.

We passed through two negro villages of considerable size. Madison, a small stop on the A. and W.P.R.R., consists of a group of shanties and a small shed—depot, about as large as a waiting shed on a Northern Ohio traction line. An amusement park adjoins the village and affords such pleasure as rope swings and impromptu merry-go-rounds.

We later passed two churches and a school, the latter of a style of architecture surpassing most northern rural schools.

One village clustered around a combination saw mill and cotton gin. The chief industry evidently operated by a middle-class white, who lives nearby.

The well-graveled highway speaks well for the roads of Montgomery county, but the condition of the wooden bridges, spanning several small streams is far from satisfactory.

Our return was made in time for dinner and justice was done by the substantial dinner.

Company C Briefs

1st Sergeant Robert Yeend who had been removed to the field hospital has again joined the company.

The 136th M. G. Battalion will stage a minstrel show in the future. Company C band will have prominent place in the arrangements.

Captain Siddall has made arrangements for banking small sums for those who so desire it.

Corporal Fred Long banged one squirrel on his Friday morning hunting trip.

Company C band has arranged for four nights practice each week. Monday, Tuesday, Thursday, and Friday.

A machine gun range has been located about twenty miles from Camp Sheridan. This range will be used by the 134th, 135th, 136th M.G. Battalion. The location is east of the Alabama river.

Those transferred from Company C to other units have taken up their work in their outfits.

Musician Leffel, 6th Ohio, a bass, will assist Company C band.

The Ravenna Republican:
Thursday, October 18, 1917
Portage County Boys Buy Liberty Bonds

Bonds to the Amount of $7,200 Taken by Ninety-six Members of Company C—Visitors from Other Commands—Other News from Portage County's Company

By Charles M. Conaway

Oct. 15, 1917

The offer of bonds for the Second Liberty Loan to the officers and men in the service of the United States has created considerable interest and enthusiasm among the units of the 37th Division and especially Company C, 136th M.G. Battalion.

A meeting was held Tuesday of last week of the officers and men of the 147th Infantry (formerly the Sixth Ohio) and the 136th M. G. Battalion, for the purpose of explaining the object of the bonds and the advantages attached to their purchase. Patriotic music was furnished by the 147th Infantry band and the meeting was in charge of the chaplain of that regiment.

Major Parker of the headquarters' staff was the principal speaker and spoke of the value of the bonds as securities and of the great service rendered to the country by men now in the service offering their financial support.

Major Parker said that these bonds were backed not merely by deposits of gold or silver in the treasury at Washington, but by the wealth and resources of the entire country and offered the safest investment procurable at this time. The return is not a large one, but at this time each and every man has given up more financially than the interest on the security will ever amount to.

It is their value as a pledge to the country that every officer and man is willing to add his dollars to his services, that makes them a great force in the present crisis. Statistics offered show this to be the most expensive war ever waged. England's daily war expenditure being about thirty million, that of France about twenty million, and Germany's about the same as that of England, while it will cost the United States vastly more than any of these.

The speaker further stated that a free democracy was the only kind of government for all peoples and that the Kaiser must be made to realize it. In no other way can this be fully proven but that each man in the service purchase one or more of bonds.

Colonel Howard, of the 147th, closed the meeting by stating that he, "Had a little change up north and would put it to work for Uncle Sam," adding that he would open the campaign by buying $2,500 of bonds.

The canvas of this company by First Sergeant Robert Yeend has resulted in subscriptions amounting to $7,200, by ninety-six of the members. Each purchaser feels that he has laid up something for the future and against the time when he will be released from the service.

On the Company Street

Corporal Charles Baldwin and Private Raymond Summers are working in the 136th Exchange during their spare time.

Various members of the company have entertained visitors from other commands recently. Ravenna boys who have called include Lieutenant Arthur Dawley, Second Ohio Field Artillery; Corporal Paul Jones and Private Ford Barrett, Headquarters Company, First Ohio Field Artillery; William Swager, Fifth Ohio Engineers; Carl Lane, Company H., 5th Ohio Infantry, Hugh and Freeman Mahan, Fifth Ohio Engineers; Private Hasely, 5th Ohio Infantry, Private Frank Creque is making arrangements to handle the amateur photographic work of the company.

The use of a small building has been secured and will soon be in shape. At present, the quarters of Trixie, Company C mascot, are used as a laboratory by the ambitious photographer. A change will be welcome, as an increase of working space will be secured.

The semaphore signal practice of the company is in charge of Sergeant Walter Simpson, and under his guidance rapid progress has been made. A working knowledge of the hand semaphore is a necessity to our work and Captain Siddall is making every effort to bring his command up to the standard required.

A "bear" race was a part of the athletic program of last week. Much amusement was created by the sight of the entire company circling the drill field on all fours. Frank Creque was considered as being more than a success as an imitator of the dromedary or "desert creeper."

The members of the company eligible to vote in the Ohio elections next month have been registered. According to the *Montgomery Journal*, "The woman's suffrage and prohibition issues will be of great prominence."

Captain Siddall treated his company to a short hike Tuesday afternoon. The command moved as a column of fours with an advance party including flanking scouts, to guard against surprise attack. The advance detail was in charge of Sergeant Simpson and numbered eight men, including Corporal Minnick, Privates Brode, Dunning, Baxter, Cole, Cannovino, Price and Anderson.

The vigilance of the detail was attested by the fact that the main body was led directly to a pasture field in which a large black bull was pastured. The entire body was saved only by the peaceful disposition of the bull.

They are deserving of praise for leading us directly to several persimmon trees, a treat peculiar to the southern states and a treat to the Ohio boys.

The Ravenna Republican:
Thursday, October 18, 1917
Will Take Ballots to Camp Sheridan

County Board Receives Instructions to Prepare Ballots and Deliver Same in Camp Sheridan

The Deputy State Supervisors of Elections received a communication from Secretary of State William D. Fulton, Wednesday, with instructions to prepare ballots and absent voters' supplies and appoint one of its members to deliver the same in person and conduct the election at Camp Sheridan, Montgomery, Alabama, for Portage county voters now in the military service at that point. Such appointees must be prepared to leave on the instant and must be in Montgomery so that the election can be held on Monday, October 22, on which date all Ohio soldiers in that camp will vote. Special transportation facilities have been arranged by the Secretary of State for the representatives thus appointed by the various boards in the state. The expenses of the trip are provided for by a special state fund recently authorized, but the compensation for services must be paid by local boards.

Deputy James M. Knapp and Clark F. W. Filiatrault were chosen to make the journey.

The Ravenna Republican:
Thursday, October 18, 1917
Pickaninnies and Alabama Wild Cats

Letter from Ravenna Boys at Camp Sheridan Gives Impression of Dixie

In a letter to his parents, Mr. and Mrs. P. E. Krieble, Emerson Krieble of Company C 136th M. G. Battalion, at Camp Sheridan, Alabama, writes in part:

Received the precious gift I had been looking for since you wrote me you sent it. Mama, when I opened that treasure box, it looked as good to me as a box of shekels looked to pirates of old. The loaf of home-baked bread certainly did touch the spot. You folks have no idea how easily it masticated after my being used to the coarse army rations. And say, those cakes faded like snow in Alabama. I must say the "eats" brought back to memory the little house on the corner I call Home.

I suppose you are having some cold weather up there. This climate certainly is changeable. It is hot in the daytime and we nearly freeze at night. I got up this morning feeling like an icicle. But, believe me, none of us feel cold long. Every morning before breakfast they double time us for a quarter of a mile. You have no idea how much better a person feels if he takes a morning run. It gives you an appetite worthwhile.

We now have two full hours of exercises every day. We play leap frog for the whole line of the company. You will have some idea what it means when I tell you we have to jump over 170 men spaced about four feet apart. Another stunt is to get down on all fours and walk like a bear.

You asked me if we have athletics. We certainly do. I watched a game of football today between the College of Alabama and a company team. The score was 7 to 0 in favor of the college. We have real football here. This camp contains baseball and football stars from many of our northern colleges. We have a company next to us representing twenty-seven colleges. They certainly give us nice music. Nearly the whole bunch can play some stringed instrument.

This camp is surely up-to-date in all ways. It is absolutely sanitary and will furnish many comforts when completed. Speaking of sanitation, everything in the garbage line is burned. Everything is so thoroughly taken care of that there is no chance for the breeding of germs.

Sunday we went on a hike and foraging campaign. Peanuts grow plentifully here, but they sell them at five cents a sack. You can't imagine how the people soak the soldier. We Ohio boys are making them rich.

Whatever you do, don't worry about your boy's treatment. He now smokes a corn cob pipe and eats army goulash without blinking an eye. It is now ten P.M. You can hear the wildcats over in the thicket. It gives you that creepy feeling that stands the hair on end.

The Ravenna Republican:
Monday, October 29, 1917

Company Moves Camp—Captain Siddall Serves on Board—Private Enterprises—Three Receive Promotions

By Charles M. Conaway

Oct. 22, 1917

Company Notes

The past week in the Ravenna section of the big Ohio camp has been one of little or no drill but of many interruptions.

Following a half day of drill Monday morning, the Company was lined up in the afternoon, according to rank and the payroll for the month of September was distributed. The officers' mess hall was used for this purpose. Forty-five privates of the first class received their extra three dollars at this pay.

Tuesday morning the entire outfit was again lined up and each man carried his slip to the field hospitals bearing the data of his typhoid and small pox vaccinations where the first innoculation for paratyphoid was administered by medical corps physicians.

Two more shots, to be given at ten day intervals.

Company Moves Camp

The work of moving our tents and equipment to the new location, one street to the east of our old location, was carried on Tuesday afternoon (not unhampered by lame arms caused by the innoculation).

Company C is now housed or rather "tented" in twenty-one tents and accommodations are such as to allow sleeping quarters for the enlarged Company. The tents are placed ten on one side of the Company street and eleven on the other, the two rows facing each other and the arrangement leaves a court or park of considerable proportions between them. The approach to the street proper is a roadway some ten feet in width, and includes a rustic bridge, constructed under the direction of Sergeant Royce Hubbard. An extension of the rustic bridge fence from each end of the bridge shuts us off completely from the outfit next in line.

The effective use of the picks and shovels provided by Sergeant Anderson resulted in a leveling of the street and in a more artistic looking drive and parts through the low-lying section. A favorable opinion of these useful tools is being entertained by all of us, due to a closer relationship.

Along with moving day came the sides and floors that make our tents into winter quarters. This boxlike arrangement is sure freedom from dampness during the rainy seasons and helps materially in keeping the quarters. An issue of regulation stoves, made later in the week, are being put up for use and each tent will be made comfortable and homelike as possible.

A larger cook stove has been constructed in our mess hall and feeding the company will be made easier and save time.

Captain Siddall Serves on Board

Captain K. T. Siddall was chosen as one of the three officers chosen to sit as an investigation board in the matter of the death of Private Coughlin at the hands of Sergeant Hudgins, of the military police. Sergeant Hudgins was found guilty of criminal carelessness following the shooting of Coughlin late Friday night. The circumstances of the shooting are that Coughlin was riding one the automobiles used in the city camp transfer service and that Hudgins fired his revolver while halting the machine in the performance of his duty, hitting the former.

Coughlin was a member of the 148 Infantry and came from Cleveland, Ohio. He was a son of Mr. and Mrs. J. T. Coughlin of that city and was but nineteen years of age. Sergeant Hudgins came from Cincinnati.

A Number of Private Enterprises

Private enterprise is in the ascendancy in this camp. Any amount of money-making schemes are being tried out and all are achieving a measure of success. Thomas Jones and Mark Cummins have established a shoe repair shop and are filling a much felt want in that line. Davis and Saunders have opened up a first-class hand laundry and are competing successfully with the overtaxed city laundries. Clyde Reed, LeRoy Jones, Wm. Trexler and Dustin are engaged in the cleaning and pressing of military garments. Roy Lauver, Sergeant Haas and Frank Creque are all establishing themselves as photographers to the camp.

Three Receive Promotions

Corporal John Byers has been promoted to the rank of Sergeant, and Private Max Miller and Clifford Block, a new man from the Coshocton Company, have been promoted to the rank of Corporal.

First Sergeant Robert Yeend and Sergeant Joseph Carter have been recommended by their company commander, Captain Siddall, and have taken the preliminary examination for promotion to the grade of second lieutenant. Both are men of ability and have discharged their duties as non-commissioned officers in this company in such a manner as to deserve the distinction.

C Company Briefs

Non-commissioned officers' school was held last Thursday afternoon, and they were given an opportunity to inspect a machine gun at close range. All were impressed with the usefulness of the weapon.

Barnum & Bailey circus showed in Montgomery Thursday afternoon. A great many of the Company flocked to town in the afternoon and evening to attend.

Members of the outfit report gains in weight from eight to twenty pounds since our arrival.

Fourteen new men have been added to the Company the past week. They came from the first Ohio Infantry, with headquarters in Cincinnati.

Mules and horses are due to arrive this week to completely outfit the battalion in that respect.

Saddler Forrest Pemberton has been transferred from Company A, back to this company.

Intensive training period begins the latter part of this month.

A physical examination was given this Company Friday morning, dealing with the condition of the heart and lungs. None of our members were found deficient.

Private Harold Mott is suffering from an inflamed throat and the members of his squad were quarantined Friday and Saturday.

Musicians Myers and Fleishman furnished music and an escort to and from the mess hall playing, "Hail, Hail, the gang's all here," "Yankee Doodle," and other catchy modern airs.

A new schedule is in effect in the 37th Division, Reveille is at five-thirty A.M. and retreat at five P.M., giving us an earlier rising hour and more time between mess and taps.

The Ravenna Republican:
Thursday, November 8, 1917
Latest News from Camp Sheridan

By Charles M. Conaway

November 4, 1917

Today—Sunday—marks the close of the first week of the intensive training period outlined for the units comprising the 37th Division, U.S. Army. Activities have quickened during the past six days to keep pace with the general program inaugurated throughout the entire camp. The main theory of the training period being, of course, to fit the members of the former Ohio National Guard for foreign service in the least possible time and to ensure that they will be able to meet actual war conditions without a long period of similar work abroad.

Lectures on various subjects pertaining to the health of the command and also deeper and more intricate branches of the military are included in the training. Lieutenants Hubbell and Rew gave interesting and instructive talks during the week.

It is said that the present war is to be won by athletes rather than by men skilled in the military and new physical training methods are being tried out and every encouragement given to all athletic games and contests. The special ability of each man in the various branches of athletic behavior is sought out and encouraged.

Company C boasts of one or more headliners in practically all of the leading sports and this was demonstrated on Wednesday, October 24 when a field meet was held on the parade ground on the 136th battalion, the three companies of that battalion. The events carried off by our outfit included the baseball game, a close contest with a score of 7 to 5; the tug of war, the centipede race, and the one hundred yard dash. In connection with the hundred yard dash it is to be added with pleasure that Earl Price, Ravenna, received the blue ribbon which gives him the championship of the entire 37th division in this field and Howard Swartout, Kent, the red ribbon, entitling him to second honors.

Six men are to be selected from the company to take a special course in boxing. Clarence Baxter was the first of them to be selected. New equipment for furthering this sport has been bought and forms a nucleus for an open air gymnasium for the use of the company. A number of impromptu boxing bouts were staged in the company street Saturday morning and were watched by an enthusiastic audience, including the company officers. The buglers, Myers, and Fleishman, staged a round contest as did Boak and Jones of Kent, Baxter and Huff, Hubbard and Creese, Carter and Simpson, and a number of others.

Distinguished Visitors

The company was honored Friday evening by having as guests at mess, twelve of Montgomery's prominent men, including Dr. Hutchins, formerly of Oberlin College and now engaged in YMCA work here on the cantonment, and Judge Barnard, a member of the Supreme Court of Alabama. The visitors spent an hour with the company in the various squad tents, getting acquainted and giving short talks.

It was the good fortune of *The Republican* representative to meet Judge Barnard and hear his comments upon the Ohio troops and other topics. Judge Barnard was formerly a resident of Troy, a city of some 1500 population located south of Montgomery, and has been a member of the State Supreme Court for three years.

The judge expressed himself as being pleased with the conduct of the affairs of the state of Alabama since prohibition came into effect and noted the decrease in crime in the state as recorded by the court dockets of the city and circuit courts. He also added that we would soon see a dry Ohio. As to the good conduct and morality of the Ohio boys, he stated that the police dockets showed a decrease of one-fourth the number of cases entered since our arrival here. A cordial invitation was extended to the Company to visit the capital and view the things of historical interest on exhibit there. Judge Barnard praised the film production, *The Birth of a Nation,* highly and stated that it had been shown in practically every southern city during the run and that absolutely no feeling of race hatred had been brought about by it. His attitude toward the Ohio Board of Census whose ruling kept the film out of the state for so long was that the members of the board were grossly ignorant of real conditions surrounding the film.

A Ravenna Visitor

John Eastock, formerly of Ravenna, and now with the Akron company of the old 8th Ohio, brought a visitor to our camp Sunday. Rex, formerly owned by C. B. Stidsen, Ravenna photographer, was greeted by the company with as much enthusiasm as another would have been and his dog-ship was made royally welcome. Rex will be remembered as a playmate of Trixie, the Company C mascot.

Company C Briefs

The second inoculation for para-typhoid was given Thursday and the company given a full twenty-four hours for complete recovery.

The quarters of Captain Siddall and Lieutenants Cope and Hubbell are being remodeled and made ready for winter use.

The summer bathhouse has been converted into one for winter use by the addition of windows and stripping lumber and will be further improved by the installation of a hot water heating apparatus.

Private Harold Mott is recovering from the attack of throat trouble which caused him to be removed to the base hospital and expects to return to his company soon.

Monthly muster was held Wednesday, October 31, and the payroll has been signed for the month of October. A pay day will be due November 5 and may be expected any time thereafter.

The Kent members of the company have been enjoying a number of boxes of dainties and tobacco received during the past week. A few of the Ravenna contingent seem to feel that they are being neglected by the populace of their hometown.

Privates Trexler and Slavin have taken up the study of telegraphy and are building an experimental line connecting their respective quarters.

The Ravenna Republican:
Monday, November 19, 1917

A Word from Captain Siddall

Writing to his father, Judge I. T. Siddall, of the Portage county common pleas court of Ravenna, Captain Kingdon T. Siddall of Company C, 136th Machine Gun Battalion at Camp Sheridan, Montgomery, Alabama, says he is giving instructions to 172 men and five lieutenants besides attending officers' school three hours per day and conducting a non-commissioned officers' school one hour each day. Under such circumstances, he has had little time to write to his friends.

He tells of fine weather and of the peculiar southern charm of the city of Montgomery with its stately old families and everything so unlike the hustle and bustle at our northern cities. He says the work as machine gunners requires such mathematical work, some of it very close and exact, and that they are busy with angles and degrees, etc. Some of the problems are very knotty and he thinks the boys of old Company M are very fortunate to get into this branch of the service.

The Ravenna Republican:
Monday, November 26, 1917
With Our Boys in Camp at
Montgomery, Alabama

Southern Roads—Southern County Fair—Trip to Selma—Visit with Coburn Minstrel Troupe—Basketball, Football

By Charles M. Conaway

November 21, 1917

A number of the company have taken advantage of the splendid weather we have been enjoying down here and have taken several automobile trips to points distant from Montgomery and the camp.

It has always been the opinion of many northerners that the roads of the south are not of the best and that they have undergone little improvement since the Rebellion. It is the point of the *Republican* representative to correct this erroneous impression.

It must be admitted that the highways of the south have not been carefully laid out by experienced engineers as have those of the Buckeye state, for their origin is that of trails and paths rather than intentional planning. This is well illustrated by one street in the city of Troy, Alabama, bearing the name of Tree Notch Road. This street forms a section of the route followed by General Andrew Jackson his way to defend New Orleans, in 1814, and marked by him by notching the trees along the line of march.

The so-called graded highways have a width greater than that of Ohio roads and are graveled with a kind of sand and gravel that admits of easy packing and forms a permanently hardened surface.

The Pike County Fair drew several parties from Company C to the city of Troy, some fifty miles south of Montgomery.

Troy is located at the center of agricultural district in which the farmers have taken up the raising of peanuts and soy beans on a large scale. The peanut has become a mighty factor in the financial recuperation of the south since the demand for all its products has become an important substitute for butter and spreads having sugar as their chief ingredient, peanut oil is used as a cooking substitute for lard and the peanut vine is used for rough forage and is an important factor in the cattle-raising industry. Soy beans are raised to increase the acreage of rough feeds and promote dairy farms and cattle ranches.

Those of us who attended the Pike County Agricultural Fair were treated to a sight. The exhibits were excellent and included much blooded stock.

A Trip to Selma, Alabama

Sergeant Frank Elgin, Carl Elgin, Cook William Conway, Clair Dunning and *The Republican* representative motored to the city of Selma, fifty miles west of Camp Sheridan, last Tuesday to meet Mr. Elmer Elgin, father of the Elgin brothers. Mr. Elgin is touring the southern states with the Coburn minstrel troupe and had arranged with his sons to meet him there, as the closest point to Montgomery touched by the organization.

Our party was made to feel at home with the Coburn players and a pleasant hour was spent behind the scenes visiting with the star, Charlie Gano, and others.

Through the courtesy of the Coburn management we occupied choice seats at the evening performance and each of us felt himself carried back to Lake Brady at the closing months of last summer when this popular minstrel show began the 1917–18 season and incidentally its nineteenth consecutive year on the road. The entire show has been worked over and many new acts added, as well as new scenery and stage effects.

Charles Gano, a black face comedian, is taking better than ever to his role of cook in his comedy act, "The Darkytown Submarine Chaser."

Outdoor Basketball

An outdoor basketball court has been constructed by members of the company and practice games are in order among the devotees of that sport. First Sergeant Yeend, Privates Reed, Trexler, Leon Hill, Baxter, Kennedy, Shanley, and Sergeants Byers and Hubbard and Herts are among the aspirants.

Football Rivalry

A schedule of football games has been arranged among the various regiments and battalions in the division and C Company has put two teams in the field in order to determine who shall make up the 136th M. G. Battalion team.

The Ravenna Club outfit is the nucleus for the first eleven and includes eleven members of this famous Ravenna organization. Baxter, G. Smith, W. Smith, Cannavino, Leroy Jones, Leon Hill, R. Hill, Minnick, Trexler and Lindsey, making up the personnel. In addition to these Thompson, George, Swartout, Shanley, Price and Ed Gilson have reported for practice.

The second eleven is in process of formation and will be on the field in a few days. Lieutenant C. R. Cope has charge of the organization of this team.

Company C Briefs

Lieutenant Cope and Sergeant Byers have their racing car out of the garage again and have created considerable stir around the battalion headquarters with the trim machine.

Privates Harvey Williams and Quay Norman have been promoted to the rank of first class private.

A device called the "double deck" has been created by Artificer Hollabaugh and permits the use of two cots placed one above the other in the manner of railroad or steamer berths. The arrangement gives about double the room in each tent.

Several attended the polo game at the 137 Artillery drill field today. This is a game new to the majority of the Ohio troops.

A wildcat of considerable size was exhibited on the company street today by some visiting Infantry men. They had captured the animal near the camp.

Eleven privates of Company C have been excused from one trick of kitchen duty as a reward for proficiency in the international Morse code for signalling.

The Ravenna Republican:
Thursday, November 29, 1917
Camp Sheridan Boys Getting Realistic Drill

Training Now More Nearly Confined to Maneuvers Made Necessary by Actual War Conditions—French Warfare Studied—Visit to "No Man's Land"

By Charles M. Conaway

November 26, 1917

The activities in the busy Ohio camp are quickening day by day to keep pace with the lightning changes on the British and Italian fronts, and the program of training in effect is dealing more and more with real wartime conditions.

C Company is changing gradually from close-order drills to more specific work dealing with their branch of the service. The number of hours devoted to lectures and instruction are being increased and the men are responding to the change by showing an increased interest.

Special instruction in using bombs and hand grenades is being given by Lieutenant Rew and Sergeant Simpson, who are detailed to receive instruction from the French officers assigned to this camp.

A feature of each day's drill is a short hike, led by Captain Siddall, and taking in distances from two to five miles.

A hike participated in by the entire 74th Infantry brigade, including the 147th and 148th Infantry regiments and 136th Machine Gun Battalion, was the feature of Friday afternoon. The route of the march was through the infantry, artillery and engineer's camps and led to the so-called "No Man's Land," now under process of construction for the purpose of instruction in actual trench warfare. The brigade was thrown into a column of companies and the earth works were inspected by each company in turn. The field is laid out in a succession of shell holes, machine gun pits, trenches, wire entanglements and the like. C. Company was commanded by First Lieutenant Chas. R. Cope and Lieutenant Clyde Rew and to these officers belong the distinction of leading the company "over the top" for the first time. All of the company present on the hike were impressed with the methods of trench warfare outlined.

Captain Siddall, Lieutenant Cope, Lieutenant Hubbell and Lieutenant Rew have proved themselves able instructors in map reading, trench tactics, sanitation and kindred subjects and are kept busy during their hours off drill attending officers' school and conducting the school for non-commissioned officers.

The government issue of rations is being reduced to the field rating by a gradual process of eliminating the less substantial articles of diet and substituting plainer and more convenient ones. This change is felt less in our Company, perhaps, than in some of the others, due to Cook William Conway's abilities in conserving certain articles and utilizing this savings in buying fruits, sweets, relishes and dainties.

Rumors have been current to the effect that our battalion will receive a new issue of woolen clothing in the near future, including overcoats, O. D. coats, O. D. breeches, etc.

Supply Sergeant Anderson has just made an issue of O. D. (olive drab) coats and of woolen blankets and promises more clothing in the future. Barracks bags have also been issued to the men and will be used as containers for clothing when the time for our departure comes.

An Epidemic of Pneumonia

Camp Wheeler, Georgia, the cantonment used by the Alabama state troops is suffering from a serious epidemic of pneumonia, several deaths having occurred there during the past two weeks. Special precautions are being taken here at Camp Sheridan to prevent a serious spreading of the disease and only a few cases have been reported.

Orders have been issued providing for extra rations, including hot chocolate, soup and a double quantity of butter in an effort to check the epidemic. The orders also provide for increased ventilation in the sleeping quarters, prohibit doubling up of two men under one set of blankets at night, prescribes the night clothing to be worn and other preventive measures.

A special guard is posted each night in the company street to ensure that these orders are carried out and that all fires are out at taps, as the stoves are claimed to be one of the causes of colds and similar ailments.

Chilly Weather

A great many of the Ohio troops have expressed themselves as having entertained the belief that we were shipped to the southland for training in order to escape the severe northern winters, but that the government seems to have made a miscalculation in that respect.

The truth of the situation is that while the days are comparatively warm and enlivened by cheerful sunshine, the nights are abominably cold. Heavy frosts are in order and a thin coating of ice on the bath-house floor has caused more than one careless individual to measure his length on the floor. An hour of setting up exercises each morning tends to lessen the chilliness of the atmosphere and cause a general shedding of coats and sweaters.

Ohio State—Auburn

The Ohio State—Auburn foot ball contest was one of the most important as well as the most talked of grid-iron contest ever staged in this part of Alabama. The game was witnessed by a vast throng made up of both soldiers and civilians and numbering supporters of both colleges in their ranks. C Company was represented by a large contingent of Ravenna and Kent football enthusiasts headed by Captain Siddall and were more than repaid by their interest by seeing the former Ravenna High star, Fritz Schweitzer, in action.

The game was a tie at the finish.

Special Thanksgiving Services

The Wednesday before Thanksgiving Day is to be given over to the battalion field meet in which a number of picked athletes from this company will compete.

Visits Company

Harold Mott, a patient confined in the base hospital, spent Sunday with his friends in C Company and hopes to be with us in the near future.

The Ravenna Republican:
Thursday, March 21, 1918
Spring Sees Increased Activity in Many Lines at Camp Sheridan

Grist of Interesting Gossip That Tells What Our Boys Are Doing—Battalion to Have Band—Many Going Home on Furloughs—Fishing Good on the Tallapoosa

By Charles M. Conaway

March 18, 1918

The Ravenna Republican:

Baseball is now the big issue in camp athletic circles. Basketball, football, track work, all have given way before the ping of springtime sports. Elaborate schedules have been arranged in almost every section of the camp, ranging from the big stuff, regimental and battalion, to sectional rivalry between platoons and even single quads.

Perhaps the greatest boon for the national sport is the arrival of the Cincinnati Reds in Montgomery for their spring-training period. Soldiers' Field, the official camp athletic grounds, has been selected for their training grounds and localizes what is more than a passing interest.

Saturday afternoon the Reds met the team from the University of Alabama. It was the first game of the season for both organizations. Christy Mattherwson, helmsman for the Reds, worked out the best of his pitching material.

A schedule of battalion games has been arranged and C Company is holding an honorable place.

Aroused by the common spirit, the second platoon of C Company challenged the remainder of the company through their sergeant, George Moon.

Sergeant Byers accepted with alacrity, organized a team and defeated the challenging platoon by a score of four to three. The pitching ability of Dennis Swartz, of Suffield, was a strong point in favor of Byers' team.

Pay Day

Last Saturday was a joyful one for the men of our battalion. The regular monthly pay was distributed. Debts were cancelled and a general exodus for the city was made.

A Transfer

Private William Trexler has been transferred from our outfit to the field signal battalion as an operator. Trexler is a hard worker and deeply interested in his line of work.

Furloughs

A large number of C Company men are home on furloughs and a number will leave during the next few days. A leave of absence can now be secured without the demise of an obliging relative or the serious illness of a dear friend.

The Battalion Band

We are finally going to have a battalion band. The present success attained by the organization is due to the efforts of Bugler George Fleishman of Ravenna and Private Charlie McMullen of Cincinnati who have made every effort towards a successful beginning. Fleishman is acting as leader and will probably accept the post permanently.

Captain Siddall, Company C, is lending every encouragement to the enterprise.

The personnel of the organization has been strengthened by the addition of several excellent players from C and other companies. The present table of organization is as follows: Bugler, George Fleishman, Company D, cornet; Chas. McMullen, Company C., drummer; Mark Cannavino, Company C, bass drum; Jack Rock, Company C, cymbals; Barnell, Company D, cornet; Conway, Company D, bass; Bugler, Amos Buck, Company A, trombone; Amelio Chickeno, Company C, clarinet; Joe Rufi, Company C, alto; Walding, Company D, alto; Lackey, Company C, tenor; Damicon, Company C, baritone; Edward Gilson, Company C, saxophone, Williams, Company D, saxophone. Two clarinet players from K. Company, 137th Infantry have also been secured.

A concert has been arranged for at "Y" 58 on next Friday evening under the auspices of leader Fleishman.

Battalion Hike

This battalion participated in an all-day hike Friday. The men carried heavy marching equipment and stood the test well.

Canteen

A new exchange (Canteen) has been opened in the building occupied by the former battalion exchange. The establishment is under private ownership.

Fishing Trip

Buglers Fleishman and Gray, Mechanic Leroy and Private Conaway enjoyed a fishing trip over last Saturday and Sunday along the Tallapoosa River. They returned with a considerable sized catch and the usual line of stories relative to what they should have caught.

A New Cook

Private George Davidson has been promoted to the position of cook to succeed Carl Elgin who will take his place in the ranks. George is our old navy service man.

The Ravenna Republican:
Monday, April 15, 1918
Many Lines of Activity at
Camp Sheridan, Alabama

Liberty Day Celebration—The Cold Snap—Range Work—Made Mess Sergeant—On Furlough at Base Hospital, Assists at Maneuvers

By Charles M. Conaway

Camp Sheridan, Alabama, April 13, 1918

The biggest event in which the Buckeye Division has participated since its arrival at Camp Sheridan was the Liberty Day celebration of Saturday, April 6. The event was a parade through the streets of the Alabama capital and was witnessed by a crowd numbering several thousands.

Practically the entire division took part in the mammoth parade, led by Major General Charles G. Treat and staff. The units were reviewed by Governor Henderson of Alabama, and staff and passed the reviewing stand in the following order: General Treat and staff; headquarters troop, 37th division; 74th infantry brigade, including 147th and 148th infantry and 136th machine gun battalion; 73rd infantry brigade, including 145th and 146th infantry and 135th machine gun battalion, the 134th machine gun battalion, attached to divisional headquarters; the 112th field signal battalion; 62nd field artillery brigade, composed of 134th, 135th and 136th field artillery units.

It is of special interest that much attention was drawn to the various machine gun outfits by reason of the mule drawn ammunition and gun carts. The science of machine gunnery is comparatively new and developments are watched with interest by civilians and soldiers alike. It must be remembered that it has been but a space of three-and-a-half years since the Hun introduced the machine gun to the world in large numbers.

The closing event of the day was the unfurling of the large flag presented to the state of Alabama by the people. The flag was unfurled by General Treat on the south lawn of the capital building. Governor Henderson and others made patriotic speeches.

The Cold Snap

Montgomery and vicinity has experienced the coldest weather, for this time of year, that has ever been known, during the past week. The men at camp have experienced little discomfort as a little additional clothing soon solves the problem.

Range Work

Our battalion has had some interesting experiences on both the machine gun and pistol ranges the past two weeks. The "dough boy" outfits started their range work several months ago but the M. G. outfits will soon be on a level with them in the matter of experience.

The pistol work is done on the divisional range. Some excellent scores have been made by Company C men.

Made Mess Sergeant

Private First Class Dewey Dustman has been appointed mess sergeant for C Company, succeeding Frank Elgin, of Kent. At the time of the change one corporal was reduced to a first class private and Privates First Class Ruggieri and Richison were reduced to the rank of private.

On Furlough

Private Chas. Sanders has returned to his home at Ravenna for a few days on account of his mother's illness.

Private Alva Rice was called to his home at Dayton, Ohio, by the death of his father, William Rice. Mr. Rice formerly resided in Ravenna.

A telegram from Sergeant Moon, whose home is at Kent, announces he is seriously ill and is unable to return at once.

At Base Hospital

Musician George Fleishman, Ravenna, Private Ervin Theiss, Cincinnati, and Sergeant Walter Simpson, Kent, have been removed to the base hospital during the week. All are suffering from sickness brought on by the sudden change of weather.

Returns to Company

Private Robert Lindsay returned Friday from the base hospital. His illness was due to poisoning by exposure to Alabama vegetation.

Acting Clerk

Private Harold Boak, Kent, is acting as company clerk in the absence of Corporal Miller, furloughed home for nine days.

Assists at Maneuvers

Lieutenant Harold Hubbell, Ravenna, and Captain William McCord, Canton, acted as observers at the maneuvers of the 74th infantry brigade on Thursday and Friday of this week.

The Ravenna Republican:
Thursday, April 25, 1918
Portage County's Company Busy in Montgomery Activities

Working Out Series of Maneuvers—Much Interest in Visit of Birdmen—Improving in Markmanship— Grip Epidemic

By Charles M. Conaway

Camp Sheridan, Alabama, April 20, 1918

The 74th Infantry Brigade has been more than busy for the last three days of this week working out a series of maneuvers. The ground covered was the drill and parade grounds adjacent to the camp and some of the rougher spots of the reservation. The work was under the personal direction of Brigadier General Gaston and staff. The 147th and 148th Infantry Regiments, the 136th Machine Gun Battalion of the 74th and one battalion of the 62nd Artillery Brigade and a detachment from the 112th Field Signal Battalion were the units employed in the open warfare problems worked out.

Brigadier General Gaston but lately succeeded Brigadier General McMaken, following the discharge of the latter from the service, as commander of the 74th.

An Informal Visit

Monday of this week the camp welcomed several visitors of an unusual nature. The callers were several aeroplanes of different types from nearby Taylor Field, the government aviation camp located south of Montgomery.

All day Monday the planes circled overhead, taking in the sights about camp. However about two o'clock in the afternoon, a real thrill was furnished when one of them alighted on the drill field of the 147th Infantry.

The machine was piloted by Second Lieutenant P. V. Hoffman who was accompanied by Mechanic Smith. The lieutenant was on his way to visit a sick friend in the base hospital.

Following recall a crowd trooped over to see the "wonders". The Taylor Field birdmen's arrival in the camp is the second appearance of flyers here, the first being the flight of Ruth Law in behalf of the Second Liberty loan.

On the M. G. Range

Companies C and D, this battalion, were on the machine gun range Monday of this week. A considerable improvement in the effectiveness of the fire of individual gunners is noted.

Receive Discharge

Honorable discharges have been given to the following officers of the 135th: First Lieutenant Stewart B. Hays, Company C, formerly of Coshocton, O.; Second Lieutenant Roland R. Smith, Company B, formerly of Canton, O; and First Lieutenant Howard L. Bible, Company A, formerly of Coshocton, O. Each of these former officers leave behind him a splendid record for service with the battalion.

On Furlough

Corporal George H. Smith returned to his home at Ravenna on Monday of this week, called there by the serious illness of a relative.

At the Base Hospital

Private Harold Boak has been taken to the base hospital on account of serious illness.

Private Emerson Krieble and Kenner Smith returned from the base last week.

An Order on Furlough

An order has been issued from the headquarters of this battalion to the effect that there be no more attention to furloughs and that no man in this organization shall apply for an extension.

Grip Epidemic

The grip epidemic, which is going the rounds of camp and city alike, is taking its toll in C Company along with the other outfits of the battalion.

Granted Furloughs

The following left the company Thursday evening on nine-day furloughs to their respective homes: Sergeant Walter Simpson, Kent; the Hill brothers, Leon and Raymond, Ravenna; Mechanic Chas. Leroy, Ravenna; Private John Kennedy, Atwater; Private Forest Pemberton, Ravenna and Private Carl Gless, Ravenna.

At the Coliseum

The week's offering at the Sheridan Coliseum is *Very Good Eddie*, the New York success of a couple of years ago. A score of C Company men were present Thursday night.

The Ravenna Republican:
Monday, May 6, 1918
Company C Returns from a Five
Day Warlike Hike

Real War Conditions Simulated and There Are No Laggards—Liberty Day Observed—Tribute to YMCA Camp Locals

By Charles M. Conaway

Camp Sheridan, Alabama, April 29, 1918

The 74th Infantry Brigade returned Sunday from their five-day hike to the government aviation station at Taylor Field, near Downing, Alabama.

The brigade left camp Wednesday morning early with these outfits in line: the 147th Infantry, the 148th Infantry, the 136th Machine Gun Battalion, the 147th Ambulance Company, and a detachment of the 112th Field Signal Battalion.

Brigadier General Gaston was in command at the start but called back to camp to take command of the 37th Division when General Chas. G. Treat was ordered to the Western Department. His place was taken by Col. Galbraith, 147th Infantry, who brought the brigade back into camp at the close of five days.

The brigade moved in full marching order, each man carrying the full pack containing a shelter half with pole, rope and pins, a change of clothing, one blanket, a poncho, mess gear, emergency rations, toilet articles, etc. Combat and wagon trains accompanied each unit and the machine gun battalion were equipped with the usual gun and ammunition carts, mule drawn. The ambulance company included a number of their motor driven ambulances in their equipment.

The First Halt

The first permanent halt was made near the Montgomery Shooting Club, about nine miles from camp, where camp for the night was made. The hikers arrived at the campsite about noon. "Pup" tents were put up at once, picket lines put out for the animals, and preparations made for cooking a warm meal at suppertime. Most of the men took advantage of the proximity of a small creek to remove the accumulated dust of the day despite a rumor that the stream was connected with an alligator swamp of huge proportions.

This first camp was located in a sandy stretch of untilled land and many and varied were the snakes and lizards found among the blankets of the unhappy sleepers before morning.

It fell to the lot of C Company to furnish the battalion guard Wednesday night and the luckless ones who had been on "sentrygo" found Thursday's hiking a little stiff.

At Taylor Field

The start for Taylor Field was made bright and early Thursday morning, but before we had covered the twelve miles to the next camp the march assumed the proportions of a "forced march," but our customary good spirit prevailed and the machine gunners developed neither stragglers nor quitters.

We pitched camp just east of the aviation camp proper. While near the station the men were treated to the sight of a number of flights by the embryo flyers and the work of one "stunt" plane in the hands of an experienced aviator whose control of his machine was wonderful.

To add to the variety of camp and field experience it began to rain shortly after our arrival and soon the streets were a sea of mud.

Prompt work with entrenching tools made everything high and dry in short order, however.

Observe Liberty Day

While in camp Friday, a program was rendered in observance of Liberty Day by the men and officers of the brigade. The following exercises were carried out: Introductory, Colonel Galbraith; 147th Infantry reading of President Wilson's proclamation by Lieutenant Farse; short address, Captain Wicks; music by the 147th Infantry band; singing by the men of the assembled organizations.

Following the regular program vaudeville skits were presented by local talent of the several outfits.

Field and Athletic Meet

A brigade athletic meet was held Friday afternoon in which representative teams from the two infantry regiments, the machine gun battalion, and the ambulance company competed.

The events won by the 136th M.G. included the 100-yard dash; the centipede race; the 220 yard dash; machine gun "in action" drill.

The winners of the centipede race were from C Company, captained by Private Lee Damicon, Ravenna. Lee's racers held the division championship and are willing to take on all comers.

Our battalion won second place in the meet, with thirty points. The 147th Infantry won the meet with fifty-seven points.

The Last Halt

Our last halt was made on a plantation near Montgomery. The campsite was adjacent to a small stream, making it convenient for man and beast. The hike from Taylor field was a matter of eleven miles but was made during the coolness of the morning hours and in fine time.

The finish of the hike wasn't under the most auspicious circumstances for the last five miles were made through a violent rain and wind storm and not a little mud. When the advance pulled into camp just before mess time Sunday, everyone was in great spirits.

A Tribute

For the benefit of the curious it is well to add that men were never fed finer than our battalion and company while "hitting the road" and credit is due the cooks of the several outfits.

The Army YMCA

If those who subscribed to the recent appeal for funds for the Y could have seen these workers in action during this hike, which is a fair sample of real war conditions, they would have doubled their subscriptions.

The "movies," the singing, and the facilities for writing letters couldn't be bettered.

We echo the sentiment of every man in the service when we suggest "three cheers" for the Y and their workers.

Camp Locals

First Lieutenant Harold L. Hubbell left Monday night for Ravenna to spend a ten-day furlough with his parents, Mr. and Mrs. Chas. Hubbell. Lieutenant Hubbell is justly proud of his recent promotion.

Mrs. Willis Lutz, Millerburg, Ohio is visiting in Montgomery with her husband, Private Lutz, Company C. Corporal Shanafelt and

Private McCay have returned from the base hospital after a short confinement there.

Private William Gray is spending a nine-day furlough at Ravenna.

Mrs. Ed Gilson, of Ravenna, is visiting her husband, Corporal Ed Gilson, for a few days.

Waggoners Shirl and Jesse Marsh, headquarters Company have returned from furloughs spent at Ravenna.

The battalion lost an excellent officer when First Lieutenant C. R. Cope resigned and returned to his Ravenna home.

Battalion baseball, Privates vs. Noncoms, won by Privates by a thirty-seven to six score.

❖　　❖　　❖

LeRoy—Moniet

Mechanic Charles V. LeRoy of Company C, 136th Machine Gun Battalion, and Miss Mary Moniet of Rootstown, were married, Saturday evening at the home of the officiant, Reverend Father C. J. Clamcy of the Ravenna Church of the Immaculate Conception. The groom returned to Montgomery on Tuesday evening and the bride will live with her mother, Mrs. Mary Bradley, in Rootstown. The groom is a son of Mr. and Mrs. James M. LeRoy of Lincoln Avenue.

The Ravenna Republican:
Monday, May 13, 1918
Weekly Letter from the Camp Sheridan Boys

Saturday Field Inspection—Musical Four—Acting
Sergeant Major on Leave to Camp
Gordon—Promotions—Several Have Furlough

By Charles M. Conaway

Camp Sheridan, Alabama, May 8, 1918

Following their return from the brigade hike the 74th Infantry Brigade settled down Monday to the usual camp routine of drill and the company streets are again the centers of activity. The first days of the week were spent cleaning up the camp, tents, stables, and everywhere and all personal equipment had to be scoured and washed to a condition of spotlessness.

Saturday Field Inspection

The event of the week was the divisional inspection held Saturday forenoon on the drill grounds adjacent to the Wetumpka Road just outside the city. The inspection was of field equipment or equipment "A." Shelter tents were pitched and personal equipment laid out accordingly. Field kitchens were set up and field cooking equipment put in place and checked over.

Personal equipment was checked in each organization. The inspection was to represent that of a brigade in the field and the campsite was laid out accordingly.

A Musical Four

Three members of Company C are coming into prominence in a musical way. Musician George Fleishman, Privates Thereon McCay and Erwin Theis and Musician Amos Buck, Company A, are appearing frequently of late at the different YMCA huts. Private McCay is pianist. Theis is a vocalist, while Buck and Fleishman play the cornet with more than ordinary ability. They also made a hit as a quartet.

Acting Sergeant Major

Sergeant Lester Roller, C Company, is acting as battaliion sergeant major following the transfer of W. J. Treavitts to Company D as sergeant.

136th Defeats 146th

The 136th Machine Gun Battalion is putting a strong team in the field in the Buckeye League and are out for honors in camp baseball circles.

The 146th Infantry met defeat at the hands of the 136th Thursday evening by a score of 3 to 1.

They play the 147th Infantry team Sunday afternoon.

Heath—Lackey

The marriage of Miss Jessie M. Heath, daughter of Mr. and Mrs. Ivan Heath of Richmond, Ohio, and Private John Lackey, Company C, took place April 22 at Richmond while the groom was on furlough. Private Lackey is well-known in Ravenna and Kent, although a resident of Lima. He was formerly manager of the Ohio City *Progress*.

On Leave in Camp Gordon

Private Raymond Summers and Musician George Fleishman spent the week end at Camp Gordon, Atlanta, Georgia, visiting with the former's brother, Leslie "Smoke" Summers, in camp there. Smoke is attached to the base hospital there.

On Furlough to Ravenna

Sergeant Elmer Schultz, Camp Stanley training camp graduate, and Supply Sergeant Harold Anderson are home on furlough at Ravenna.

Promoted

Corporal Harold Haas, Kent, headquarters company, has been promoted to the rank of sergeant. He will be made personnel sergeant and handle the paperwork of the battalion.

Attached to Company

Sergeant George White, 112th Sanitary Train, has been attached to C Company. Sergeant White is a Leon Springs graduate and will be commissioned at a later date.

Sergeant Don Watkins, 112th Sanitary Train, has been attached to B Company similarly.

Acting Supply Sergeant

Private John Lackey is acting in the capacity of supply sergeant in the absence of Sergeant Anderson.

On Furlough to Kent

Corporal Ivan Shanafelt has been furloughed to Kent for nine days to visit his parents, Mr. and Mrs. W. A. Shanafelt.

Sunday Dinner

Speaking of eats, if certain unmentionable stay-at-homes back in Portage county could only have seen, much less partaken of C Company's Sunday mess, they would have run themselves thin getting to the nearest recruiting place.

A fine "feed" of roast pork with all the attendant fixings wasn't enough. Mess Sergeant Lynn Dustin trotted out great helpings of strawberry shortcake, served with whipped cream.

The Ravenna Republican:
Thursday, June 20, 1918
Visited Camp Lee

Sheriff Joseph Jones, wife and little son Jim visited their son, LeRoy Jones, in Company C 136th Machine Gun Battalion, at Camp Lee, Virginia.

The young soldier is expecting orders at any time to leave Camp Lee and the country. They found him in good health and in good spirits.

They also found Captain Kingdon T. Siddall of Ravenna back with his old Company M boys. Captain Siddall, who is the only son of Judge I. T. Siddall, had just returned from the hospital at Camp Sheridan, Montgomery, Alabama, where he was confined by illness for several weeks. He recently completed a course in a military school that made him eligible for a higher commission, but preferred to remain with his boys whose training had been in his hands from the first.

Camp Lee has a varying population averaging something like 40,000 boys in all stages of training.

Camp conditions were found to be excellent. While their daily military duties are stiff and strenuous, they are cheerful. Hard work and intensive training is the rule of the day, but right and restful recreation is provided.

The visitors were very much impressed with the work of the YMCA and the Knights of Columbus, in wholesome evidence throughout the big camp. The privileges given them by these splendid organizations is appreciated by the boys, who find the home atmosphere cheerful.

The "Hostess House" is another invaluable auxiliary in the social life of the camp and its problems.

The Ravenna Republican
Monday, July 15, 1918
Portage County's Company at Last Arrives Overseas

Word Has Been Received That Company C (Old Company M) May Be Now on the Firing Line—All Portage County Wishes Them Well

Word has been received of the safe arrival in France of Company C, 136th Machine Gun Battalion of which Captain Kingdon T. Siddall, only son of Judge I. T. Siddall of Ravenna, is in command.

Portage County War News

Writing from overseas, LeRoy Jones, son of Sheriff Joseph Jones, tells of his safe arrival with Company C, 136th Machine Gun Battalion and says he is enjoying La Belle, France.

Judge I. T. Siddall has received two letters from his son, Captain Kingdon T. Siddall, the first of which was written on ship within sight of the shores of England. He said the trip was long and monotonous and without special incident save a violent storm and a submarine scare without the "sub." Writing later from France, he said the air was clear and bracing and conditions generally good. He spoke in particular of the frugality of the people and of their earnest devotion to the cause of their country. Company C, of which he has command, has been transferred to the 4th Army Corps, but is not yet on the firing line The 133rd Regiment with which Lieutenant Edgar W. Maurer of Ravenna is identified, has been transferred to Italy.

The Ravenna Republican:
Thursday, August 8, 1918
Portage County in the War

Correct Address of Our Own Boys Overseas—
What Are They Doing?

Sample address for boys of our Co.
Pvt. John Doe, Number . . .
    Company C., 136th Machine Gun Battalion.
      A. P. O. No. 763,
        American E. F.

Note: Be sure to have number correct. Be sure to have A.P.O. No. 763 correct. Be sure to spell out American.

Sheriff Joseph Jones received a postal from his brother, William Jones, telling him of his safe arrival with the colors in France.

Writing from La Belle, France, Private W. F. Gray, son of Mr. and Mrs. H. E. Gray of West Highland Avenue, told them of his safe arrival. He said they had a fine trip with only one storm which gave him a genuine taste of *mal de mer.*

After landing in France they were sent straight to a rest camp.

He said that two things impressed at first landing: one of which was the fact that there were nearly eighteen hours of daylight. The other was the universal presence of stone houses instead of wooden ones. ". . . that we see in good old United States." He says it is hard work to write because of the censor and for his friends to write to him whether they hear from him or not.

Writing to his parents, Sheriff and Mrs. Joseph Jones, while en-route to France, Leroy Jones, who is with Company C, 136th Machine Gun Battalion, says under date of July 4:

It certainly is an ideal day, one of the nicest we have had on our trip.

The YMCA is even found out in the ocean and besides furnishing the fellows with writing materials and books, provides movies for the evening entertainment. Religious and other meetings are also in they day program of this spendid organization.

"This ocean is somewhat of a joke. If one uses soap with it to wash clothes it sticks to the garments like gum. I started to wash my legging before I knew about it and then I couldn't get the soap off of them. . . . We celebrated the 4th on board and one officer made an interesting talk in which he told us of actual doings at the front."

He said that while he had enjoyed the trip very much, he would prefer traveling by rail. He saw large fish jumping out of the water and some claimed they saw two big whales.

Writing from La Belle, France, on July 7 he told of his safe arrival and that he was then in a small rest camp which he expected to soon leave. That was on Sunday night and he said he had been on guard all night up to ten o'clock Sunday morning. He says that daylight lasts until ten-thirty P.M. and it is light at four A.M. He continues:

The country around here is very pretty and is slightly hilly. The wheat crop has not yet been harvested, but looks good. The fields are very small, all less than an acre. They are cultivated in every corner. Many of the men, women and children wear wooden shoes and you can hear them stomping along a block away. They have splendid horses, Belgian, I guess, and all of the French people have heavy-wheeled wagons and when the load is heavy they drive tandem. I saw three being driven that way today. I haven't seen a buggy yet. The children all want pennies, I guess that is all they can say, although I did hear several small children singing, "Hail, Hail! The Gang's All Here." Lots of little boys not much larger than babies ask for cigarettes, the word for which is the same in French as in English.

Everything is high here except wine. The saloons are kept open on Sunday and are run by women. On the boat little oranges cost one dollar per dozen and one had to pay fifteen cents for two bananas.

Everything is high. . . . There isn't anything much here to spend money for. We are not allowed out of the camp. . . . It is eight o'clock and the sun will not set for an hour yet. . . . One of the first things I saw after landing in France was one of the Browning Locomotive cranes. It was right near the gang plank on our boat. We haven't drilled any since we arrived here and don't think we will. Our ball team beat one of the English teams this afternoon. We have a pretty good team now.

The Ravenna Republican:
Monday, September 9, 1918
Portage County in the War

Various Items of Interest Concerning Our Own Boys Who Are in the Service

The following letter is from Corporal Emerson Krieble, Company C, 136th Machine Gun Battalion:

France, Aug. 9

Dear Dad, Mother and Kiddies:

Yesterday seemed to be the happiest since in France. I got mail to the amount of eight letters. And believe me, it's the first reading matter I've had in over six weeks.

We are now in the trenches, and there's where I've been since hitting this sector. We have an emplacement somewhat away from the rest and see little of the outside world.

This morning we started cooking our own meals. We are going to have SOME dinner—hamburgers, tomatoes, potatoes, bread, coffee, jam and last but not least, good country butter. It sells here for about sixty-five cents per pound. That isn't bad. There are two very scarce articles in this country—eggs and meat. Eggs sell at ten cents (per one) and meat's out of the question.

We certainly have lots of noise around here. There are artillery pieces all around us. Last night, we watched four Fritz planes trying to get over our lines. They surely met some opposition from machine gun and shrapnel fire. This morning two planes were fighting above the clouds. All that we could tell of it was the hum of the machine guns in them.

After a couple of nights here we were welcomed by the enemy with a shower of gas. The alarm was spread all through this sector, but I don't think much of it reached us. Dad, it is some sensation to have one of those cages on and know, or think you know, that there is an

104

enemy outside of it waiting for a chance to get into your system. But all of us know there is absolutely no harm if you have one of the American masks on. Wish you could see the French respirator—it's slow death itself.

Say, Mama, when I get back I'm going to introduce a new scheme in the plan of housekeeping. It does away with chicken coops, cow barns, etc. The idea is to have them all in one. The last place we billeted the people lived in one room, the cow and horses in another and we lived in the hay mow. You see when you want to milk, just chase the cow into the kitchen and go to it.

Well, Dad and Mother, I must close for this time. Now don't worry about me. I'm satisfied and so are the rest of the fellows. Here's hoping the Hun meets his Waterloo soon and then we can have a long interesting talk.

Your son,
Emerson

The Ravenna Republican:
Monday, September 30, 1918
Captain K. T. Siddall Writes from France

Boys Will Push Gigantic War to Speedy and Successful Conclusion He Says

Judge I. T. Siddall has received a letter from his son, Captain K. T. Siddall, under date of August 8. "Somewhere in France." Captain Siddall says:

We have made many moves throughout France and each is a source of great responsibility to a commander. Transportation is both scarce and slow and hikes are necessarily long, but all are sticking to the game and working like tigers.

France is enchanting and the French know it and are fighting for it. We have lived in small villages in shell-torn houses and barns that exude all the *perfume de cattle* that centuries of occupation by *genus bovine* have developed. I have felt quite well ever since arriving. All of the men are in a splendid state of health and we shall certainly give an account of ourselves over here.

I was the first in the battalion to get into real trenches, having been sent to reconnoiter for the organization.

it is interesting to see how quickly the boys became assimilated to the ever-changing conditions of life over here. They like to be in the trenches better than back in training cars. All have been in the trenches and under shellfire, but details as to the occupation cannot be divulged.

During all of this period I have been in command of the battalion and I have never worked so hard or assumed so much responsibility in my whole life. There is an unending amount of night work and we all have become veritable owls. All is work, work, work, in a determined endeavor to push this gigantic war to a successful and speedy end.

You must not worry about my health or welfare, for I have not been sick a day, and we are going to keep the Boche on his defense from now on. We feel confident of entire support from home, and with that and our determined energy this thing cannot drag on as it has in the past.

You have no idea how fortunate the boys who enlisted at Ravenna are. As it stands today, they are together continually to a man. They know each other and they have an *esprit du corps* which I think is unrivalled.

Now for a bit of the France I have seen. The vistas are long and superb. The roads are in perfect condition. They wind over all the country and their white surface, fringed with populars can be seen for great distances. Crops are enormous, but they are cultivated and reaped by hand. The American farmer and his harvesting machines can well take lessons from the French. All the land owners and farmers live in villages close by their lands.

Captain Siddall's address is: 136th Machine Gun Battalion, A.P.O. No. 763, American E.F.

He explains that the A.P.O. means Army Post Office and that *American* is written out to differentiate from *Australian* E.F.

o   o   o

Kent Soldier Killed in Action

Corporal Ivan W. Shanafelt of Kent has been reported in the list of those killed in action.

The Ravenna Republican:
Thursday, November 7, 1918
Germany Gives Up

Accepts from General Foch the Terms of Armistice Imposed by the Allies—News Received Here This Noon—Arch Enemy Recognizes Hopelessness of Situation and Surrenders

News of the surrender of Germany by acceptance of the terms of the armistice imposed by the Allies was received here this noon. Bells are ringing, whistles are blowing and the greatest news of the century is being celebrated in a manner worthy of its magnitude and worldwide significance. Once more the people are called to rejoice over the tiding of peace and this time it is a sure announcement. Civilization has won and the world has been made safe for democracy.

Ravenna Boys Good Soldiers

Captain Kingdon Siddall Says There Are None Better Anywhere

Judge I. T. Siddall received a letter from his son, Captain Kingdon T. Siddall, November 5, written at the war front in France on October 30, in which he lauds the soldierly qualities of the boys from Ravenna and other Portage county towns who have been under his command and whose military conduct, he says, has been equal to that of tried veterans. He wishes the fathers and mothers to know the calibre of their boys at the front who have shown themselves to be effective, brave and reliable from the first great drive in which they participated and acquitted themselves with characteristic heroism and efficiency. He spoke in highest praise of their conduct when called upon to go over the top. He was of the opinion that the war would not end before the summer campaign of 1919, although he saw some reason to hope that it might terminate any time. He said that the Germans are playing for more time in which to reorganize their shattered armies to continue the fight against civilization.

The letter was written before the collapse of Austria-Hungary and of Turkey and the series of swiftly moving events that have been blazoning the pages of world war history in the past few days.

The Ravenna Republican:
Monday, November 11, 1918
World War Ended Today

Germany Signs Armistice and Hostilities Cease at Six O'Clock This Morning—News Officially Announced from Washington—Kaiser Wilhelm, Hun Menace Forever Removed—Ravenna Will Celebrate Tonight

The world war ended at six this morning by the signing of the armistice on the part of Germany. Word was given to the country at two-fifty this morning by the State Department at Washington and at four AM Mayor Bert Redmond received word of the news by telephone from Cleveland. At the earliest possible hour the *Cleveland News* had copies of its *Official Peace Extra* on sale in Ravenna streets, followed by *Plain Dealer* extras.

Again the courthouse bell was rung by Caretaker David Stockman who invited all who wished to participate in this act of heralding the news to climb the tower stairs at the courthouse and go to it. For upwards of two hours the bell that rang out the tidings of the surrender of LEE in 1865 and that has called the citizens together on all momentous occasions for upwards of seventy-five years, proclaimed the fall of the HUN and the triumph of world democracy. The bell at the Riddle Coach and Hearse plant also rang out the news, and everybody prepared to join in demonstration that would dwarf that of Thursday when it became known that Mayor Redmond was planning a big celebration that evening. It was therefore decided that work would continue throughout the day at the factories and workshops, the stores remain open, and there should be no suspension of business anywhere.

Celebrate Tonight

Ravenna Will Hold Big Peace Celebration Tonight—Let Everybody Turn Out

Firing of the cannon will begin about seven o'clock this evening at which time all citizens of Ravenna and Portage county are invited to assemble at the court house front to join in a grand parade, headed by the Ravenna city band. Bring along anything not dangerous or harmful with which to make a noise, but please bear in mind that guns, revolvers and firearms are forbidden. Everybody is urged to carry an American flag.

The Ravenna Republican:
Thursday, November 28, 1918
Soldier Mail Arrives

A large amount of overseas mail arrived this week, relieving suspense and anxiety in many homes, some of which had received no word from over there since September. Word comes that letters in earlier mail had been burned during the intense action of the 37th Division of which old Company M is a part as they were in up to the close of the hostilities.

The Ravenna Republican:
Monday, December 2, 1918
Killed by High Explosive Shell

Chas. M. Conaway Writes Particulars of Death of His Friend, Clair Dunning

In a postscript to a letter dated Belgium, November 8, Chas. M. Conaway writes of the death of Clair Dunning as follows:

Sergeant Hentz informs me that I may write to you about Clair. Perhaps you may have heard already.

Clair was killed at the beginning of our drive here by a high explosive shell. The concussion killed him. Death was instantaneous.

Clair had all the nerve in the world. Too much nerve, almost. All of his commanders say he was one of the best soldiers in the Company.

You know how I must feel about it. My best friend is gone now and I am alone. Everything will be different from now on.

We were inseparable here as at home.

He was killed while crossing a road during the advance.

Captain Siddall secured a chaplain and gave him a Christian burial. I was not lucky enough to get to see him before he was buried. No doubt the captain will write back the details to his people. It is terrible and the end is not yet.

Private Chas. Conaway
Company C, 136th Machine Gun Battalion,
American E.F.

Under date of Oct. 27, he writes as follows:

Belgium, October 27, 1918

Dear Folks:

Will try my best to write something like a connected letter for once, now that we are semi-permanently located for a day or two.

We have been too much on the go for much letter-writing for the past few weeks.

Just now we are billeted in a town and pretty decently fixed. Anyway, we have a chance to rest and clean up.

On our way here I saw the work of the Hun devils here in Belgium. Ruined cities, ruined farms, everything ruined. Certain sections are completely wiped out. The grass can't even grow. Trees are all shot off or cut off.

We passed through one of the sections where the heavy fighting of the early days of the war was done and there isn't a thing left. Everything blasted right off the face of the Earth. Back home when we read about all this we were inclined to say that the magazine writers exaggerated. On the contrary, they didn't and couldn't begin to tell the half of the real story.

Since the Germans have been chased out, the Belgium refugees are pouring back into their homes and an abandoned city is full of life and people almost overnight. And just as soon as they settle in their former homes (or what is left of their homes) they begin to do what they can to reclaim the farm land.

Tell John and Howard they ought to see these people work dogs to wagons. They pull real loads, too.

Private Chas. M. Conaway, 1524197

Company C, 136th Machine Gun Battalion,

American E.F.

The Ravenna Republican:
Thursday, December 5, 1918
Captain Siddall Wounded

Judge I. T. Siddall received word Wednesday from Washington, that his son, Captain Kingdon T. Siddall, of Company C, 136th Machine Gun Battalion, had been slightly wounded in France.

According to word received in home letters written by members of the Company, Captain Siddall had previously been gassed by the Huns and was taken to a hospital. It is supposed that he had recovered from the effects of the gas and was again with his Company when wounded.

The Ravenna Republican:
Monday, December 9, 1918
Young Hero Dies for His Country

David M. Murphy, Member of Old Company M, Killed in Action

Mr. and Mrs. George M. Murphy of Van Burean Street received a telegram from Washington, Thursday officially confirming the news that their son, David N. Murphy was killed in action on October 31.

The Ravenna Republican:
Thursday, December 19, 1918
Boys All Like Captain Siddall

So Writes Roy Jones to His Parents, Sheriff and Mrs. Joseph Jones

Sheriff Joseph Jones received a letter from his son, Roy Jones, Sunday, who is with Company C, 136th Machine Gun Battalion, "Somewhere in France" in which he stated that he was well and OK. The letter bore the date of November 7 and said he expected to remain in the town where he was billeted for a day or two.

The letter was a great relief to Mr. and Mrs. Jones as this was the first letter they had received from their son since the signing of the armistice. They feel now that they have good grounds to hope that nothing has befallen him. Rumors of his death and again that he had been captured and was a prisoner in the hands of the Huns, were rumored for a time and while no confirmation of the reports was ever received, they were disquieting to the family. He says:

Much has happened since last writing you, but I am feeling well and everything is OK with me.

Was sent in advance of the Company to locate billets and a place for the kitchen and the train. Didn't have much trouble getting room for the fellows, as we were the first American soldiers the Belgians had seen and they were sure glad to see us and were anxious to do whatever they could for us. We expected to be there for two or three days, but the next morning we were to leave that afternoon for the front to participate in another drive. We left at 4 o'clock and arrived at the front about four in the morning. We slept in an old barn all that day and about midnight left for the positions closest to the Germans. A short barrage was put over between five and five-thirty and after it was lifted we started forward. He said that they met pretty stiff resistance and did not go very fast, but that at the end of the first day they were within a few hundred yards of their first objective.

Our platoon was supporting the first wave, and stopped at a Belgium farm where the people had just churned. The Germans took the butter but we got the buttermilk and some sweet milk. While our boys were driving the Germans from that vicinity the people hid in straw stacks and it was there that we first heard of our losses. They sure did hit us hard, and I have thought of it a good many times since. You will probably hear about it shortly after you get this letter. Four of the fellows were good friends of mine.

The second day was easy, as the Germans had fallen back, but on the third, fourth, and fifth days we could do nothing but hold, as we were on the banks of a canal from which the Germans shelled us during those three days and we sure were lucky. My squad was the last one in our Company to be relieved, and it was after twelve o'clock when we left, getting back to the kitchen about two o'clock. We started back after supper and an hour's rest, and hiked until about seven-thirty in the morning and ate and rested in a chateau. We left there about nine AM and hiked until about 10 PM when we arrived at this place. . . . This town is a fairly large one: the largest one in which our battalion has yet been billeted. We have been here a day-and-a-half and expect to be here a day or so. We hear we will go to Italy and also to England but all that is rumor.

Captain Siddall is back from the hospital and there isn't a man in the company who isn't overjoyed to see him and who wouldn't do most anything for him.

Bill Trexler was over to see us today. He is looking good and is still in the Signal Battalion. Slaven was also here to see us.

Have had five or six letters from you since last night and about a dozen others. I don't know when I shall get them all answered as we are very seldom in one place long enough to do much writing.

I am not bothering about souvenirs, for I think if I get home, you will have as good a one as anybody; for believe me, a fellow who sees active service over here and comes out OK and can go home when the time comes, is sure a lucky boy and the greatest of all souvenirs.

I have a pair of wrapped leggings taken from a German officer which I will try to carry until I get something smaller and just as good. The way most of us figure is that we have enough to carry without the stuff that a low, degraded German would wear or use. But, of course, it is interesting to those at home who don't see that stuff as we do.

About every other German is a machine gunner and after he has fired his last shot at you or is surprised at his post he will hold up his hands and cry, "*Kamerad!*" and then will go on to say that they didn't know they were fighting Americans.

Our boys say that they won't take any prisoners but when the time comes they haven't the heart to kill them.

The flu seems to bother most everyone and everyone takes a chance of getting it.

Your son,
Roy Jones

Company C Fought on Four Fronts

Saw Action in Lorraine, Argonne, St. Mihiel and Flanders

The following letter was written by Sergeant Emerson Krieble of Company C, 136th Machine Gun Battalion, the first to be received by his parents, Mr. and Mrs. P. K. Krieble, since the signing of the armistice:

November 24, 1918

Dear Mother and Dad:

This being the one day set apart for Dad, or Father's Day, I'll make it both for Father and Mother.

At present we are located in a little Belgian village called Desselghem. I'm writing in one of those little Belgian kitchens pictured in many of the American storybooks. The large fireplace will be found in nearly every home.

Since peace has come we have been hiking nearly every day and it isn't into the interior either. I want to see all of France and Belgium that is possible. We were thirty kilometers from Brussels but didn't get to see the city.

I will give you something of our movement since leaving the United States. We embarked at Newport News and landed at Brest, France. We trained in a couple of little villages near the coast, then they put us on the Lorraine front. I suppose you think this was a very active front, but it was nothing in comparison to the Argonne Forest and some more we were in. I suppose you have read of the battle. We drove the Huns for six days and it was some hellish going. There were hundreds of Boche machine guns scattered for miles.

I will fill you full of the experience we had on four fronts—Lorraine, Argonne, St. Mihiel and Flanders.

I have been receiving all your letters regularly, also the pictures.

Your son,
Sergeant Emerson Krieble

Special Requests to Be Denied

War Department to Arrange for Return of Soldiers Soon as Practicable

The Local Board of Portage County has received the following letter issued by the Adjutant General of the Army concerning two matters about which there has been a great many inquiries from relatives of soldiers and therefore the instructions are copied verbatim:

When a state of order has been restored overseas and the military situation there has improved to such an extent as to justify the withdrawal of American troops, the War Department will adopt the most effective and speedy means to hasten the return of all soldiers to their families at the earliest possible date, but owing to the immense amount of detail attached to the process of demobilization, the War Department must decline individual requests for discharge or return to the United States soldiers overseas.

"Relative to bringing home from overseas the remains of deceased soldiers, I wish to advise that it is a policy of the War Department to return to the United States as soon as practicable the remains of all soldiers who have died overseas."

The Ravenna Republican:
Monday, December 23, 1918
Ravenna Boy Dies in French Hospital

Raymond Hill, Reported Slightly Wounded, Makes Supreme Sacrifice November 7

Mr. and Mrs. Frank Hill of Number 465 South Chestnut Street, received a telegram from the War Department at Washington, Thursday afternoon, advising them of the death of their son, Raymond E. Hill, which occurred at Base Hospital Number 36 in France on November 7.

The young soldier had been listed among those who were slightly wounded, word to that effect having been received in late November from Private J. L. Klingman in which he said that Raymond was under his care. His wound greatly weakened him at first, but a difficult operation on his side and hip had done wonders and he was gaining strength.

On receipt of this letter they felt very relieved and expected that their boy would recover and come back to them. Their surprise and grief on receiving Thursday's telegram cannot be told. Letters received from their other son, Leon, on November 24, show he did not know of his brother's death at that time, but supposed he was on his way to recovery, and may not be aware of the fact at the present time.

Raymond Elwood Hill was born in Ravenna, August 3, 1894, oldest son of Mr. and Mrs. Frank Hill. He was raised in the community of his birth and after finishing his studies in the city schools found employment at the Annevar Mills when he responded to his country's call.

He is survived by his parents, his soldier brother in France, his brother, Norman, who lives at the homestead, and his sister, Mrs. Ethel Goodyear, wife of Fred Goodyear of Cuyahoga Falls.

The young defender was wounded at the front in the big Argonne fight.

The Ravenna Republican:
Thursday, December 26, 1918
Another Boy Tells of Real Soldier Life

Chester Keys Writes from Belgium—On Five Fronts and Over Top Twice

Mr. and Mrs. Lionel Keys have been relieved of their anxiety about their son, Sergeant Chester Keys, member of Company C, 136th Machine Gun Battalion. Various reports have been in circulation at one time that he had been killed in action. But the receipt of this letter dated at Desselghem, November 24, thirteen days after the signing of the armistice and the cessation of hostilities, clears away the fogs of rumor. He says:

We are billeted here for the day and as everyone is writing Dad a Christmas letter, I didn't want to be a slacker.

Well, Dad, I have been on five different fronts and over the top twice. When I say "over the top" it was up and at them right with the Dough boys. We kept after them for five days. We slept and sometimes we didn't. Our eating was about the same. Our mission as machine gunners is to keep back of the infantry, but we didn't stop for the Dough boys or anything else when we got started.

The last drive was open warfare to a finish, with nothing but hedges and fences to stop Fritz' 77s and his heavier artillery. I have been covered by mud and water thrown up by them. I have been gassed, shot at with airplanes, been through as stiff a barrage as Jerry could put up, sniped at, been through France and a good part of Belgium, have been bombed and if I missed anything, it wasn't my fault.

We rode in boxcars for days and also in trucks sans springs and seats; drank chlorinated water and shell-hole water; also drank "Betico" Vin Blanc, Vin rouge, Champagne in France and Cognac and Schnapps in Belgium. We've shot craps and played poker; cussed the Army and swore at our gas masks. We are American soldiers.

My pay lasts sometimes for two days. The money looks like so many trading stamps and has no value whatsoever except as calculated in bottles, litres, or grams. Bottles mean the juice of the grape; litres mean milk and grams either butter or cheese (when they can be had).

Of course, were I writing to a girl or to the "women folks" I would camouflage all of the real truth; but this is meant for Dad and no one is SUPPOSED to be concerned.

My delicate feet are simply ruined and now cover as much territory as four ordinary feet should. We had English shoes issued to us the last time and I took No. 9s. The English have no conception what shape a human foot should be and so simply make a covering out of what should be a protection. Their sizes run two larger than the American sizes, so Belgium has not only shell holes to fill. I am very sorry too for the treatment accorded us by the Belgians has been such that it will never be forgotten.

One reason for such an amazing letter may be that I slept in a bed last night for the first time since I joined the army. The only thing lacking now is a bath and perhaps then I can write a book.

These foreign countries seem to have completely forgotten bathing as an essential to hygiene in their education. One either uses the natural waterways for bathing or his coffee tin, more often the latter. And then one becomes so easily used to not bathing.

Another attraction I almost forgot to mention, and I must not forget the Cootie, a charming little creature about the size of a sheep tick. I found seven of them in my bosom and, Father, there are others, THERE ARE OTHERS!

The day the armistice came through we were stopped in the road as we were going on our third drive. The Doughboys came out of their holes and threw turnips at the Germans. Both sides made the night as light as day shooting flares at each other.

We have not slept outside since we stopped, though our billets are sometimes nearly open to the stars owing to Jerry's proclivity to blow things skyhigh.

Just now there is a very pretty Belgian girl showing another Sergeant the family album. He is doing his best to make himself understood and we together are doing some tall calisthenics. But we are making ourselves understood just the same.

Well, Father, I hope the war is over. As many French say, "*Finis la guerre.*" No more pup tents, few more hikes, finish blisters and ague shakes. Ague shakes are caused by a mixture of H. E. and shrapnel with doses every few seconds.

Hoping this finds you well and will close with lots of love to all.

Chester

The Ravenna Republican:
Monday, January 6, 1919
Claire Dunning Praised by Captain

Tribute to Bravery and Soldierly Qualities of Ravenna Soldier Killed in Action

The following letter was received by Mrs. George M. Dunning of West Main Road, whose son Claire Dunning was killed by bursting shrapnel in Belgium while advancing against the Germans. The letter is dated in Belgium November 12 and was read at the memorial service for the young soldier at the First Christian Church, Ravenna, Sunday, December 29.

Belgium, 12 November, 1918

Mrs. George M. Dunning
Ravenna, Ohio

Dear Mrs. Dunning:

You have doubtless received official advices of the death of your son, Claire Dunning, while advancing against the enemy in Belgium, on October 31 last at about four PM.

While no words of mine can assuage the sorrow now weighing upon you and Mr. Dunning, it may comfort you to know that he is laid at rest beside a beautiful winding lane near Thielt, Belgium, in a countryside fairer than the imagination can picture. We, whom fortune shall return to Ravenna, shall bring to you vivid pictures of the spot where the boys who gave all-in-one of the final actions, are laid in rest, and of the heroism and splendid courage which Claire displayed to the last.

No one knows of the sterling traits of manhood possessed by Claire better than you. During the period of his military life these qualities hardened into a character which will safeguard his spirit and give to his comrades an example worthy of constant emulation.

Sympathetically,
Kingdon T. Siddall
Captain Company C, 136th Machine Battalion

Ravenna Soldiers Get War Cross

Captain Kingdon T. Siddall and Lieutenant Elmer E. Schultz Decorated by King of Belgium

One hundred and fifty members of the Buckeye or 137th Division were decorated with the Belgian War Cross for "faithful and meritorious services" and for "exceptional gallant conduct in action," December 17, and were complimented for gallantry unsurpassed by any troops in the great war. The decorations were made in the name of the King of Belgium.

Among those decorated were First Lieutenant Elmer E. Schultz of the 145th Infantry, and Captain Kingdon T. Siddall of Company C, 136th Machine Gun Battalion.

Lieutenant Schultz is a brother of Mrs. Redmond, wife of Mayor Bert Redmond, and Captain Siddall is the only son of Judge I. T. Siddall.

The Cleveland Press:
Wednesday, January 22, 1919
Here Is Official List of 37th Division Heroes

The Press has received from the headquarters of the 37th Division a list of men and officers cited by Major General Farnsworth, commander, "who by their spendid conduct and devotion to duty, have especially contributed to the successful operation of the division in France and Belgium against the enemy."

The 37th Division is composed of former Ohio and West Virginia National Guard units.

The division is scheduled to arrive in New York before the end of the month. News dispatches Tuesday said the division had been ordered to embark.

The men cited are:

136th Machine Gun Battalion
Company C

Fred Demmler
(Died of wounds)
Leroy Jones
George H. Smith
Emerson Kreible
Thomas Bosworth
Joseph D. Schultz
Carl R. Hentz
Howard Swartout
John T. Maxwell
John Klinger
Leo A. Damicon
Felix Marlatt
Alva B. Rice

Rossiter Hobbs
Raymond Summers
Clair Dunning
(Killed in action)
Arthur Brode
Edward Dyer
Forest Pemberton
(Killed in action)
Harold Runyan
William Richison
Joseph Eunello
Sydney Murphy
Clyde Bender
Angelo Rosso

Mark Cannavino
George Coverdale
William R. Smith
George Sanders
Dewey A. Dustman
George P. Fleishman
Clyde Reed
Herman Blumenschein

Frank C. Creque
Edward A. Hare
George W. Parsons
Frank D. Murphy
Albert Raier
William Skilton
Thomas Rich

The Ravenna Republican:
Tuesday, January 28, 1919
Portage County in the War

Various Items of Interest Concerning Our Own Boys Who Are in the Service

Mrs. James Brode of Beech Woods has received several letters from her son, Arthur Brode, who was wounded October 31, 1918, and is now in the Canadian General Hospital at Boulogne, France.

He wrote that he was having fine treatment and care, but expected to spend New Years Day in the hospital. After an operation on his hip the wound healed nicely, also the one on his arm, while the wound on his side is still open and discharges. He thought, however, that it would heal soon. The wound in his side was very deep, requiring the insertion of drainage tubes. He said he was gaining in strength and was able to sit up a little.

In his last letter, dated December 18, he was looking forward to receiving his Christmas box from his mother, the contents of which he correctly guessed before its arrival—chocolate, of which he is very fond.

Kent Courier:
Thursday, January 30, 1919
Will Meet Company C Boys at Pier

The Ravenna Republican publishes the following of interest to Kent and the entire community:

Mayor Bert Redmond has received word from Congressman M. L. Davey in reply to his communication relative to the proposed demonstration in honor of the boys of Company C, 136th Machine Gun Battalion on their arrival from overseas, in which he says that there will be no objections on the part of the War Department to a committee of home citizens meeting them at the pier in New York.

Under date of January 25 he says:

> The 136th Machine Gun Battalion was designated to sail on January 2nd, but for some reason did not start. They were then designated to sail on January 20th and no word has been received that they have sailed.
>
> I assume that you will want to have Mayor Johnson, of Kent, join you in this movement.

The mayor and committee will meet next Saturday evening at the Ravenna city council chambers to prepare a program.

The Ravenna Republican:
Monday, March 17, 1919
Company C on Way Home with
Entire 37th Division

Left France Last Wednesday, March 12, on
Huntington—Plan for Portage County Unit to Stop at
Ravenna for Parade

Mayor Bert Redmond received a telegram from C. R. Sharp at Washington, Saturday afternoon advising him that the War Department had released the information that the entire 37th division including Company C, 136th Machine Gun Battalion is on the way from France having embarked Wednesday, March 12.

The telegram was turned over to C. R. Francies, secretary of the Soldier's Homecoming Celebration committee, who immediately wired Mr. Sharp asking him to communicate with the War Department relative to the possibility of permitting Company C to stop at Ravenna long enough to make a parade or other demonstration provided the routing from the seaboard should be by way of this city.

Kent Courier:
Thursday, March 20, 1919
Kent's Machine Gun Boys Enroute Home

Boys of Old Company M, Who Gave Good Account of Themselves on the Battle Fields of France and Belgium, to Be Warmly Welcomed

It is reported, but not officially confirmed yet, that the 136th Machine Gun Battalion, formerly Company M from this county, has embarked on the transport Huntington and will arrive at New York on March 24th and that this battalion will stop at Youngstown and Ravenna and parade. Confirmation of this report is being sought from the War Department by Congressman Davey, which we expect to have soon.

If this good news is confirmed, it is being planned by the local committee on arrangements to give them a reception at Ravenna, where they will arrive some date about the last of next week, and automobiles will be provided for conveying all returned soldiers from Kent and Franklin township.

As soon as the exact plans are learned from the War Department the committee will make further detailed arrangements through circulars carried in the daily papers. It would be of great assistance if all soldiers now returned and at home would leave their names and addresses and the service they were in with the committee.

The Ravenna Republican:
Thursday, March 20, 1919
Company C Boys Ordered to
Parade in Ravenna

Due to Arrive in New York Next Monday—Will Remain There Four or Five Days Before Starting for Camp Sherman

Company C, 136th Machine Gun Battalion, will stop at Ravenna on their way from New York City to Camp Sherman.

Definite word was received to this effect Wednesday.

A telegram was received by Mayor Redmond Wednesday afternoon from Adjutant Gen. Harris, saying that:

> Company C, 136th Machine Gun Battalion, due at Hoboken about March 24, and assigned to Camp Sherman, is authorized to stop enroute at your city for parade and reception. Battalion Commander will wire advance information as to time of arrival.

The Ravenna Republican:
Monday, March 31, 1919
Company C Expected Wednesday for Parade in Ravenna

Telegram from Captain Siddall States That Boys Are Scheduled to Leave Camp Merritt Tuesday—Bells and Whistles Will Announce Arrival in Ravenna

C. R. Francies, secretary of the soldier's homecoming celebration, has received a telegram from Kingdon T. Siddall of Company C, 136th Machine Gun Battalion, stating that the boys will probably leave Camp Merritt, New Jersey, on Tuesday and that they will stop off on their way and parade in Ravenna. He said that he would wire the exact time of departure from Camp Merritt. They should reach Ravenna sometime Wednesday. The public will be advised of their coming by the ringing of bells and blowing of whistles.

All details of the program heretofore published in *The Republican* will be carried out and everybody in the county is cordially invited and urged to come to Ravenna.

Citizens everywhere in town are asked to decorate homes and business places.

The Ravenna Republican:
Thursday, April 3, 1919
Welcome Home, Company C

Mayor Redmond Called Up from Youngstown This Forenoon and Said That Company C Is There and Will Be Here Tomorrow Morning According to Schedule—They Are Parading in Youngstown Today

The Battalion Boys will be in Ravenna Friday. This is official.

Secretary C. R. Francies of the soldier's homecoming Celebration received a second telegram from Captain Kingdon T. Siddall of Company C, 136th Machine Gun Battalion Wednesday morning informing him that the Portage county company, numbering 112 will arrive in Ravenna from Camp Merritt, New Jersey, Friday morning, at seven o'clock and they will remain until seven o'clock in the evening.

Mayor Redmond immediately got busy on receipt of the news and all is readiness for a rousing reception.

It should be understood that all who have returned from camp or overseas are included.

Mayor Redmond asks that the people of Ravenna make this a general holiday, closing all businesses. Kent has already done so by declaring a general holiday. Kent is coming enmasse and one of the biggest crowds ever seen at the county seat will congest its streets that day.

The boys, for their part, will give the people a grand parade and show them how the Dough Boys of Portage county appear in fighting trim. It will be a sight that will go down in memory.

The committee on refreshments has arranged for a chicken dinner at the First Christian and First Methodist churches for the boys. This will be followed by a lunch with hot coffee in the evening.

Anyone desiring to contribute to the dinner or lunch may take their offerings to either of the two churches on Friday morning or money may be contributed with Miss Elizabeth Haymaker at the Red Cross.

Kent Courier:
Thursday, April 3, 1919
We're Coming Back to You

By Chester C. Moreland, 37th Div. American E. F.

Many months ago we left you,
    Dear friends of Buckeye state,
To come to France and Belgium,
    To show Germany her fate.

We left you with our hearts bowed down,
    For you're folks we love the most,
Then too the trail on which we came
    Was marked by death's mile posts.

We arrived in sunny France, at Brest,
    Our voyage o'er quite "tame,"
But six weeks from the time we sailed
    Found us in the trenches—in Lorraine.

For five weeks we held the lines,
    Schooling ourselves at war,
Proving to "Fritzie" his opinion of us
    Was entirely wrong by far!

Then from Lorraine we "shouldered arms,"
    Our faces toward Verdun,
To a front which was proclaimed by all—
    Impossible—advance means doom!

The great advance in the Argonne!
    Don't you remember the time?
'Twas in the end of September,
    And your friends were there and mine!

Six days of rain, filth, shells and blood,
    Days lived in hell's own gates;
With your friends "going west," and mine,
    To save the good old states.

But you just bet your last good cent
    That for each chap "gone down," comrades
There were three of Fritzie's comrades
    Strewn on that shell-swept ground.

And Jerry would not stop!
    Tho' tired we kept up step,
And when at last relief came,
    We had learned of Yankee pep.

From the Argonne we went eastward,
    Up into Saint Mihiel,
When the Boche again were promptly taught—
    An Ohioian won't keep still!

Then little Belgium called us
    To come to her at once,
To help her and the Poilus
    Show up Germany a dunce.

At Olsene—in Belgium,
    We revived the spirit of yore,
Till on the fields of Flanders
    Lay a thousand Boche, or more.

"Kamerad, Kamerad, Kamerad!"
    Came from each of "Jerry's" men,
And a second drive was needless,
    For they knew 'twas their Amen.

It was then that news of peace came,
    The words which meant so much
To all the allied nations,
    As well as those "in Dutch."

And now we're coming back to you,
    Those of us who are left,
To share with you the happiness
    Of a world to live in rest.

We know you're glad we're coming,
    For we've tried our best to show
Just what we think in arms and deeds
    Of our Mother state—Ohio.

We love dear France and Belgium,
    But now the war is thru,
We're returning to the state of states,
    Ohio, the "Buckeye"—and YOU!

The Ravenna Republican:
Monday, April 7, 1919
Maids and Mothers Vie in Welcome to Homecoming Battalion Boys

People Quit Homes, Business Places and Farms Are Deserted and Citizens Everywhere Join in Greeting Returning Heroes—Spectators Line Streets for Miles

Friday, April 4, 1919 will be remembered as "The Day When the Boys Came Home"—when maids and mothers vied in welcoming their hero lads.

In wartorn khaki, steel helmets and packs, Portage county battalion boys came marching home and were given an enthusiastic reception by a throng of citizens that lined the way from the Erie depot, to the uptown business centers. Old Glory floated proudly from the big steel staff and the town was gay with flags and streamers. All Ravenna and Kent and county quit work, and homes, workshops, stores, and farms were deserted to be able to greet and entertain the boys who marched down Main Street on the morning of Sunday, September 16, 1917, to the old Pennsylvania depot and entrained from Camp Sheridan in Alabama, and with the exception of some who are recovering from wounds or illness, have returned from overseas and will soon be marched into private life again.

The boys of the fighting 136th, strong seasoned veterans who battled for world democracy, arrived over the Erie from Youngstown at 7:10 in the morning. Whistles began to blow at seven o'clock, keeping up their chorus of announcement, until the boys were told to "fall in" after the reville, which meant "falling out" of the cars for the parade. People hurried out of their homes, hundreds coming in from nearby precincts, while other hundreds were already here from remote sections of the county, waiting for the signal. As if by magic the streets became suddenly filled with surging crowds that lined the flag-decked streets between the courthouse and depot in numbers that spoke the one thought of the day. "Welcome Home to Portage County Soldiers and Sailors," making good the legend in big letters across Main Street. Fathers and mothers and sweethearts hurried to the train, impatient for the first glimpse of the faces they longed to see and for which many of them waited long minutes. It was a scene that cannot be woven into words and that nothing but the unwritten language of the heart can tell. And the joy of the homecoming soldier was equally beyond the power of verbal expression. "Words can't tell it," said one of the boys as he cordially grasped the welcoming hand. It was truly a homecoming song without words, the soul melody of which the poet sang. "Heard music is sweet but that which is unheard is sweeter."

Ravenna was in gala-day garb, but the skies at first seemed loath to reciprocate in kind, threatening rain and shutting out the sunlight. But as the day advanced the prospects became brighter, the omens of storm disappeared and gleams of sunshine began to break through the rifting clouds, until a more continuous illumination chased away fog and chill and dried the streets and walks.

There was a large delegation over from Kent, accompanied by Post's band of forty pieces, an organization which will soon celebrate its twenty-fifth anniversary. The Ravenna City band headed the parade, followed by soldiers, Post's band, members of the Ravenna W.R.C. and the Italian Marine band. The streets were lined with people from a point well down from Main street to the Erie depot, a distance of nearly a mile, and Ravenna has not seen a larger throng for years.

The line of march was up Cleveland Road and Sycamore to Main; east on Main to Freedom, north on Freedom to Highland Avenue; west to Chestnut; south to Main; east to Prospect; south to Riddle Avenue; back to depot where ranks were broken. Captain Kingdon T. Siddall and Mayor Bert Redmond headed the boys who marched in double formation amid the cheering.

From the depot the boys returned up town and many of them went to the Christian and Methodist churches where warm chicken dinner awaited them. Others went to their homes instead, in order to spend all of the time possible with those who have been waiting for eighteen months to greet them. The remainder of the day was spent in visiting and taking in familiar sights clothed in new character to the young heroes whose dreams of Home Sweet Home had come true.

In the evening, lunch was served at the same churches and the day closed with a dance given for the boys at the Elks' club rooms.

Thus did the boys come and thus were they welcomed.

Company C was the first organization of soldiers to leave Portage county for the big war and the only volunteer company that was raised in its territory. Enlistments were opened in the spring of 1917 and the company was mustered in as a unit of the Ohio National Guards in early summer, being then designated as Company M, of the 10th Ohio Infantry. The boys remained in barracks at Ravenna and were trained in daily drill until their departure for Camp Sheridan at Montgomery, Alabama, Sunday, September 16, 1917, 130 strong. Previous to this fifteen of their number were transferred to the Rainbow Division and left Ravenna for Camp Perry, and soon afterward to their embarkation camp and to Europe. Two of the Rainbow boys made the supreme sacrifice: Harry Puffer and Leon Mosier, both from Ravenna.

Some time after the arrival of the boys at Camp Sheridan, they were assigned to the 136th Machine Gun Battalion and were thereafter known as Company C. They left for Newport News where they embarked for France on June 16, 1918, arriving at Brest in July. Eight months later they embarked at Brest for the United States and arrived in Hoboken on March 23, after twelve days on the water. They took part in the big parade in Youngstown on Thursday with the 136th Field Artillery and the 134th, 135th and 136th Machine Gun Battalion and arrived in Ravenna on Friday morning.

Of the Company C boys who went to Brest, Claude M. Davis, Jr., and Ivan Shanafelt of Kent; Clair S. Dunning, David Murphy, Raymond Hill, Howard Bartholomew of Ravenna and Forrest Pemberton of Brady Lake made the supreme sacrifice. There is also a large list of wounded.

"It was just to our liking," the boys all said, and praised the people for their consideration in giving them all of their time in which to visit "The Old Folks at Home" as well as certain other younger folks who were waiting for them in audience of one.

Besides Captain Siddall, First Lieutenant Cyril H. Sutherland of Mansfield and Second Lieutenant Frank C. Leroy were at their posts in the line of march. Beaming over them all was the smiling face of "Cook Conway" whose surname is William or just plain "Bill" and whose happiness bubbled over at every step. The veteran chef is as proud of his boys as any mother.

Private Arthur G. Brode of Ravenna is in a New York hospital recovering from wounds; Wilbur Minnich of Ravenna and Walter Keeter also of Ravenna, William Meyers of Kent, have recovered from wounds and are back with the company.

The 134th Field Artillery with which the Battalion boys appeared in the Youngstown parade was commanded by Major John A. Logan, of three generations of "Fighting Logans" and a member of the staff of General Farnsworth. Major Franklin L. Pierce is in command of the 136th Machine Gun Battalion.

The boys had a great homecoming ocean trip, filled with fun and features that would make a good follow-up "Arabian Nights," and which none but American doughboys could originate. They worked all of the college degrees in amplified form within the restraints of army discipline and the stories some of them told would make an audience of old time Covenanters laugh.

Arriving at Camp Merritt, the monotony of the daily grind was relieved by twenty-four hour passes issued for the boys to go to Gotham and take in the sights.

The boys were in Columbus, Saturday, where they participated in the grand review of the entire division of 25,000 men who marched through the streets of the Capital city.

It is expected that all of them will receive their honorable discharges within two weeks, excepting some of the officers.

The triumphal gladness of the day was alone shadowed by the remembrance of those who are sleeping under the skies of France and Belgium where they gave up their young lives.

Portage county will never forget the young heroes who are sleeping with those who answered the last summons in other wars of the Republic.

146

Kent Courier:
Thursday, April 17, 1919
Company C Boys Happy at Home

Almost all the boys of Company C, 136th Machine Gun Battalion, have returned from Camp Sherman and are again enjoying the comforts of home.

Following is the list of those who have returned and also of those who are still absent:

At home: Maxwell M. Miller, sergeant; George Moon, sergeant; Thomas Bosworth, sergeant; Thomas E. Jones, sergeant; Howard Swartout, corporal; Dennis Swartz, corporal; Harold Boak, corporal; Willis Lutz, mechanic; Frank Elgin, cook; Harry Wilt, private first class; Johnnie Jones, private first class; John Lackey, private first class; Hubert Strayer, private first class; Carl H. Elgin, private first class; and William Myers, private first class, who was wounded.

Kennerdal George, sergeant, was left behind ill in a New York hospital.

The following were transferred to the Rainbow Division: Raleigh Merydith, Ben Sawyer, Ralph Hawk (home), Frank Ferry, Cletus Weideman (home), Mike Spangler (home).

Killed in action: Ivan Shanafelt, corporal; Claude Davis, private first class.

Among others who left with the company, but were transferred to other commands are the following: Kenneth Haas, sergeant, to the 135th M.G. Battalion; Harold Haas, sergeant major, to the 37th division headquarters; Walter Simpson to officer's training school, where he obtained a lieutenant's commission. He was not among those ordered to France.

The Ravenna Republican:
Thursday, April 24, 1919
History of Company C in
France and Flanders

Authentic Record of All Activities of Portage County's Volunteer Company from Time of Leaving United States until Return Especially Prepared for "The Republican" of Ravenna, Ohio.

By Charles M. Conaway

"Sling equipment." "Forward March."

As Major John A. Logan gave the command the 136th Machine Gun Battalion snapped into motion and we were really on our way overseas at last.

Our period of intensive training, which had extended over a period of more than a year was at an end and we were about to embark upon the great adventure to which we had been looking forward since April 1917.

Swinging out of Camp Lee, Virginia, onto the main highway, under heavy marching order, we set foot upon the trail we were to follow for the next nine months. A trail that was to lead across the broad waters of the North Atlantic, across the Republic of France to the foot hills of the Vosges mountains along the western front from the Swiss border to the North Sea and eventually back to the United States and home.

How little we knew what the future held in store for us.

In spite of the repeated admonitions of the officers that we must maintain absolute silence throughout the movement and that our own safety and the safety of others depended upon secrecy a certain enthusiasm crept into the march and it was with difficulty that some of the lighter hearted ones were prevented from breaking into song. But under many and trying circumstances in later days this desire to sing buoyed up the spirits of their depressed comrades when the miles were long and the roads were rough and the strains of "Katy" or a similar marching song wakened the echoes along the turnpike and chased away the demon of gloom.

Mobilization and Training

The 136th Machine Gun Battalion was trained at Camp Sheridan, Alabama as a part of the 37th Division, United States National Guard, and was formerly the Third Battalion of the 10th Ohio Infantry.

Following the mobilization of the Ohio Guardsmen at the Southern Camp in early September, 1917, radical changes were made in the Ohio Division with a view to creating a combat unit similar to those used by the nations then actively engaged along the western front. As a result of these changes the 10th Infantry became the 134th, 135th, and 136th Machine Gun Battalions.

Company M, made up of Portage County men, was made C Company of the 136th Machine Gun Battalion and replaced with a number of men from Co. I, 10th Infantry, Coshocton, Ohio, and some from the 1st Ohio Infantry, Cincinnati also broken up.

Major John A. Logan of Youngstown, of the third generation of "Scrapping" Logans was made battalion commander and Clyde E. T. Tousley, 1st. Lieut. Adjutant. Both officers had formerly been with the 3rd Battalion, 10th Infantry.

The 37th Division had undergone a period of intensive training at Camp Sheridan from September 18, 1917, to May 23, 1918, designed to fit them for open warfare against the time when the Hun should come out of his hole and stand battle.

During this training period particular emphasis was placed upon the importance of machine guns and machine gunnery in this, the most modern of all wars.

Accordingly every effort was made to place every type of machine gun and all available information before the men.

Practice marches, maneuvers, trench training, trench digging, range work, infantry drill, training in the mechanism of the different types of machine guns and automatic rifles, physical drill, all of these had their places in the busy days required to fit us for overseas duty.

The period from May 27 to June 21 was spent at Camp Lee, Virginia, where we were equipped for overseas duty and where we received the final touches to our preliminary training.

The time spent at Lee was largely used in range work with the Vickers Machine Guns with which we had been fully equipped shortly after our arrival there. Considerable stress was placed also on elementary trench training for at this time Chateau Thierry and Belleau Woods were unknown and it was difficult to forecast the tide of battle or to venture an opinion as to what the summer would bring forth.

Down the James River
Published Monday, April 28, 1919

Notwithstanding the urgent need for secrecy, our movement through City Point, Virginia, was generally known and our appearance was the signal for a quiet demonstration upon the part of the populace. Red Cross workers distributed hot coffee, cigarettes, and good cheer through the battalion and the streets were filled with people bent on witnessing our departure. Apparently, no one minded the drizzling rain, neither soldier or civilian, as we waited patiently for our turn on the river steamer that was to carry us to the sea.

At 11 o'clock the order came to fall into ranks and we were hurried aboard the river boat *Pocahontas* with the voices of the people of City Point wishing us God speed and good luck from darkened doorways and crowded pier.

Early Saturday morning the *Pocahontas* docked at Newport News, and we were marched ashore and to one of the parks along the waterfront. Again the Red Cross women demonstrated their ability, for in short order, we were fed up on cookies and hot coffee, the same constituting the last edible food we were to face for some weeks. The boys of the battalion certainly appreciated the efforts of the Red

Cross workers of both of the cities and the memory of their good work was carried far.

The "Cascerta"

Following the Red Cross feed, we were hustled to the waterfront through an endless chain of evil-odored warehouses and up the gangplank of the Italian-Lloyd freighter *Cascerta*.

Previous to being called into service as an army transport the *Cascerta* had served long and faithfully as a mule boat and during her better and more prosperous days had seen service as a fruit boat in the tropical service.

The *Cascerta* carried an Italian crew but was navigated under the direction of a complement of United States naval officers while the radio room was operated by American sailors.

The international mix-up aboard the *Cascerta* was wonderful, to say the least. The situation stood something like this: American troops bound for France to fight the Germans and avenge the wrongs of Belgium were traveling on an Italian-owned and manned vessel which had been chartered by the English government. British rations had been put on board in charge of an Italian quartermaster the same to be issued by an English steward, cooked by a German cook and in turn issued out to the American troops.

The armament of the craft consisted of a six-inch naval rifle at the bow and a similar weapon on the rear deck. Each gun was under the charge of a qualified gunner from the Royal Italian navy and manned by a crew of soldiers picked at random from those on board. The crew of the aft gun was made of men from Company C, under Sergeant Leo Damicon.

Further protection was afforded by a vigilant watch picked from the soldiers and placed at vantage points. This guard was posted for a twenty-four hour turn of duty and was furnished by the several units aboard in turn. In addition, a watch from the ship's crew was constantly on duty.

The Convoy Sails

Shortly after eight o'clock Sunday morning, June 23, the transport weighed anchor and pulled through Hampden Roads toward the broad Atlantic in company with six other ships accompanied by several cruisers and a host of "sub-chasers."

Once on the high seas or about 300 miles out, the war vessels steamed toward New York and the convoy proceeded alone.

When within a hundred miles of the French coast, we picked up a number of fast cruisers and were guarded carefully as we passed through the Hun infested waters of the Bay of Biscay and the southern end of the Channel.

Life aboard the transport was indeed monotonous. Life boat drill and physical exercises were the only breaks in the eternal sameness of the days.

One of the chief sports was the salt water bath provided for troop use. As a bath it was a total failure and had we been wiser it might have been taken as a warning of what we were to encounter in that line later.

Although we were disturbed by endless boat drills throughout the voyage, the enemy subs made but one effort toward us and that when we were within fifty miles of port.

Instantly warning sirens sounded and the gun crews leaped to their posts. In almost incredible time, the guns were laid on the offending craft and every ship in the convoy opened fire at once, while the cruisers put on full speed in the attempt to overtake it.

Finding that his efforts were useless the "sub" commander wheeled about, submerged, and was out of sight before the excited spectators realized either the cause of the disturbance or the danger encountered.

An Unusual Fourth

Spending a holiday on the high seas and a Fourth of July on a troop ship in time of war is a distinctly novel experience.

Dawn of the holiday found us a couple of hundred miles out and with no prospects of making land so the officers in charge called in the YMCA representative and arranged an impromptu program.

Captain Price of the 136th had spent some time in the trenches at a previous time and in a short address endeavored to impress his audience with what they were to face upon entering into the real war zone.

A short talk appropriate for the day was given by the Y worker and the affair closed with patriotic singing contributed by the husky-lunged youth on board.

France at Last

Toward noon Friday, July 5, we had our first view of France in the shape of two lighthouses looming up on our portside and giving promise that the end of our voyage was in sight.

Shortly after we entered the channel leading to the harbor of Brest. Picking our way slowly and with extreme care through the mine fields guarding this, the greatest port of entry for the coming Americans, against the possibility of a surprise from the German raiders, we steamed by the great forts and powerful guns and came to anchor inside the breakwater.

After a voyage of thirteen days we were safe in Brest harbor with the walls of the ancient city rising high up the mountain sides and evidences of American prosperity and American ability around us.

American tugs shoved us to our place along the pier; American observation balloons watched the harbor and bay day and night for evidence of a Hun raid; and an American "Blymp" or dirigible balloon sailed lazily about the harbor and environs; American stevedores unloaded the sinews of war from the many supply ships riding at anchor; American harbor boats patroled the breakwater; American bluejackets occupied the old fortress on the hill overlooking the bay for this had been converted into a training station; and last, but not least, the stars and stripes had taken the place of the Tricolor on the Customs House, the piers and everywhere that American activity had spread.

Indeed one felt that this Old World city had in some quiet, mysterious way become a part of the Great Republic itself.

After visits from the port officer, medical officers and numberless other dignitaries we were allowed to land. Commanders formed their several organizations and we set foot on French soil after the orderly manner of American soldiers wherever found.

Boche Prisoners

A single incident occurring as we were about to land, did much to repay us for the thirteen days spent on ship board and many little inconveniences, too. A hundred or so German prisoners were working on a scow heaving coal under the watchful eye of French guards and the expressions on the faces of the "PG's" were interesting to behold. Many of them were men past the prime of life, some were mere boys while the majority were husky men well-fitted for the new task they had been set to.

The answers to the questions of the German speaking soldiers on board were many and varied. Some of the ex-Huns were sullen and refused to as much as look up. While others talked eagerly. All appeared to be perfectly satisfied and as much at home on the coal barge as anywhere. They said they were well-fed and well-treated and what more could one want?

Disembarking from the *Cascerta* we turned our backs upon the sea to pursue our adventures inland for the next nine months.

Major Logan formed up the battalion in a narrow street along the waterfront and after a few words of warning as to conduct marched us off in the direction of the city proper.

After an endless climb through a maze of winding streets, we emerged into the open, back of the city. Our way had led us up an almost perpendicular hillside, the reason why the old timers had been unable to capture this same city of Brest. A man wearing armor couldn't climb the slope much less fight his way up. Later we learned that the city walls and the nearby fortress had been a bar even to the great Caesar himself when he toured Europe with his Roman bodyguard, seasons before.

154

Pontanezan Barracks
Published Monday, May 5, 1919

A hike of three miles brought us to the famous Pontanezan barracks of Napoleon. We were herded into the second floor of Number Four of the series we were told that this would be our home for a day or two and to make ourselves perfectly comfortable.

Making oneself comfortable was easier said that done. Just how Napoleon managed to keep his army around him at all much less worship him is hard to determine for his idea of barracks scarcely came up to the modern standard.

Sad to say, no improvements had been made in the hundred or so years since Napoleon's glory had faded. We slept on the same floors that the old guard had used; made our hasty toilet in the diminutive bath house adjacent and our meals were prepared in the open courtyards about the barracks. It required no particular strain on the imagination to see yourself in a cocked hat and carrying a pike.

In the after years of Napoleon's regime the place had seen service as a military prison for political offenders. A disguised gibbet gave mute evidence of the fate of many, while one section of the old wall was riddled with rifle bullets where the wretches had paid the penalty demanded by their successful opponents.

The entire place was undermined with a series of subterranean dungeons and corridors and had one been able to investigate many stories of mistaken ambition might have been unearthed.

However, the large courts made excellent places for practice of the national sport and every evening baseball held the central place of interest. The fact that darkness does not descend on that part of the world in midsummer until half past eleven o'clock and that day breaks about two-thirty, allowed the game to continue long after taps.

Officially, the period at Brest was not spent in resting up from the long voyage but actually by detail work on and about the docks down at the water front and it was a lucky youngster who did not serve on a half dozen of the freight wrestling expeditions during the five days of our stay.

Here at Brest we first encountered the overseas YMCA and owing to the strapped condition of the pocketbooks of the entire outfit the service was of little or no benefit.

The second day after our arrival a detachment of the famous Marine Corps landed and they certainly were an unfortunate bunch. Their ship, the *Henderson* had burned about 200 miles out and they had been transferred to another vessel while the unfortunate ship put back to New York. As a result of the fire and the change practically the entire outfit had lost all their effects. A local young man had been trained with this same outfit and his friends conducted a diligent search for him finding that he had been transferred over to another organization for duty at one of the American ports. A number had been lost at sea during the transfer from the *Henderson,* and it was at first feared that he had been among them.

The French Railways

After a five-day stay the battalion was marched to the railway yards near the city and our experience with the French idea of a railway began. As everyone knows Continental railroads all run opposite from the American system. Trains pass on the right instead of the left as we were always taught to expect.

The cars on the French railroads are about one-fourth of the standard American car and are divided off into compartments with a seating capacity of about eight persons. Also they have three classes of service, first, second and third, the rates varying in proportion to the service afforded. The first-class compartments are really very comfortable. The second will do and the third are unspeakable. When one travels on a continental train, he is locked in his compartment at the start off and he must be an expert tourist to make a landing anywhere near the place he hopes to go for stations are never called and half the time the train crew hasn't the least idea where they are.

But the natives of Europe feel always that they have a lifetime in which to complete a journey and the difference is small whether they stumble onto the wrong train and are carried a couple hundred miles out of the way or whether they travel at all.

Upon our arrival at the Brest yards we were counted off and assigned places in the second-class cars, eight to the compartment.

That is some of us were. The remainder about three-fourths, were crowded into third class, and the now famous box-cars. Those bearing the never-to-be forgotten legend, "Cheva 8—Hommes 40." Eight horses or forty men they carried throughout the war and the place of the diminutive French box car in carrying great loads of men and supplies are certainly important.

Next train rations were issued us. So much tinned goods for each car and this was to be doled out by the non-commissioned officer in charge at infrequent intervals. Our ration consisted of "Willie" (the popular name for corned beef) great cans of it; canned tomatoes; two small cans of English issue jam; and about forty packages of "sunshine biscuit" (camouflage for hard tack); and several cans of the great army fruit—the inevitable bean.

The Journey Inland

Finally all the preparations were completed and we rolled out of Brest with our faces to the East and the western front.

The start from Brest was made just before noon, July 11, and we arrived at Damblain, a railroad well within bombing distance of the front, Sunday afternoon, July 14.

Nothing worth recording from the standpoint of exciting incidents occurred on the way, but our route was through a most picturesque section of the country and it was midsummer hence the trip was well worth while from the viewpoint of the tourist seeing the beauties of France for the first time and from the safe distance of the railway.

After leaving Brest our way was through a somewhat mountainous section and the long, steady grades seemed to offer much resistance to the antiquated French engine that wheezed and groaned under the weight of the troop train.

As we journeyed inland we were never far from the sea as the peninsula upon the extreme edge of which Brest is located is quite narrow and the rail route skirts the north coast. At the city of Morlaix, we enjoyed a glimpse of the channel for a moment and the steamer or two in the harbor conjured up visions of far off America and brought back thoughts of home.

St. Brieuc was the next town of any size until we reached the city of Rennes. Rennes proved to be a city of considerable size and viewed from the train seemed to be a busy commercial center and railway junction.

We also passed through the American troop center, Le Mans, and found this to compare very favorably with American cities. Le Mans was long a large railway center and was, during our time in the war, the chief clearing house for troops and supplies and the center of a large district from which the American army was equipped and supplied.

From Le Mans we cut south to Tours; through Bourges; then to Djon. At Is-sur-Tille we were halted to wait for the coming of night for we were now approaching the actual front and troop movement was restricted to the cover of darkness.

This was our first experience with European methods of warfare viewed from close up and it developed that from this point we were slaves of the powers of darkness; never more to move in daylight but to sneak about from place to place like thieves of the night and to woo Morpheus during the daylight hours.

Diversion at Is-sur-Tille

Upon pulling into the Is-sur-Tille yards we were informed that the delay was to be of several hours duration and that we might make ourselves as free as the size of the place and the high wire fence about the place permitted.

A YMCA had been provided for passing troops and this furnished a center of interest especially as a young fellow helping out in the place proved to have been wounded at the front and was at that time suffering acutely from genuine shell shock.

Also a train was about to pull out for the front carrying a complement of trench veterans and their stories of the tribulations of the life were more than interesting to novices whose experiences up to that point had been few and far between. Later, we learned more of the sector to which the veterans were bound and discounted their yarns accordingly.

A lively note crept into the proceedings through the advent of a Scotch band from the British camp nearby. The Scotties entertained us with several selections and the delight of the gang was unbounded, as most of us had never seen a real live man in kilts at close range.

Also we encounterd a rarity in the form of a sufficiency of good, clean water and practically everyone availed themselves of the opportunity to shave and clean up. Of course this labeled us as rookies in the eyes of our experienced allied friends who stared through the wire at our maneuvers and it was apparent by their facial expression that they pitied us and at the same time realized that we would get away from these old ideas if given time.

The little villages and hamlets along the way presented a neat appearance in the summer sun. The houses were of stone with bright red roofs and each little dwelling had its garden spot with the neat, orderly rows of plants. It is often remarkable just how much return can be had from one of these miniature gardens when cultivated carefully. At home, one was used to broad fields and extensive, rather than intensive, farming methods and this Continental system appeared somewhat inadequate to the average Ohioan.

A common sight was the entire strength of a French family working in the fields cutting grain by hand with a sickle and tying up every straw carefully and securely, to be flailed out later by hand. Or perhaps one would see a farmer with his wife and daughter, or daughters, hitched to the plow turning up the soil at a great rate while he urged them on to greater speed. A horse and the family milk cow often pulled the wagon or the plow and appeared to make a perfectly matched team.

Always in the villages the spire of the village church towered over the lesser edifices and in much of the really war-stricken district the church and especially the church spire were particular objects of the Bosche hate. Either by shell or bomb they always managed to finish off the church first and then take up the destruction of the rest of the town.

From Is-sur-Tille toward the front many indications of the presence of the war were in evidence.

Barbed wire entanglements littered the fields and in many places the grain was growing in the midst of the defences more or less remote from the actual front line. And it was plain to be seen that the French had no intention of being caught napping again.

Here and there trenches had been dug in preparation for the expected hordes and many kilometers from the lines big guns loomed up on the mountainsides.

Arrival at Damblain

Looking about us upon our arrival at Damblain, our detraining point, we saw still more signs of war. Huge guns mounted on railway carriages stood ready to rush to the line at a moment's notice or to proceed leisurely forward, put over a few big ones and then crawl back out of range of the answering fire.

At the order to detrain we scrambled out and began righting ourselves for the hike we feared.

Finally the battalion moved off through the village proper and we were treated to our first sight of a French provincial town at close range. Just to say that the place was anything but sanitary is enough to record in these annals, but the actual appearance of the place beggars description. The appearance of the inhabitants as they crowded to the doorways of their homes was anything but reassuring.

A premonition as to how our leisure would be spent during our tour was gained by watching the efforts of several gangs of our fellow soldiers from another part of the division in the attempt to make the place halfway fit to billet in.

As we hiked on and on through several villages things showed little improvement and much of the early glamour fell away.

Billeted at Sauville

A hike of about ten kilometers brought us to the village of Sauville where we were billeted in sundry barns, stables, abandoned dwellings and the like.

In appearance, the place was identical with the others. A square occupied the center of the town, flanked on one side with the church and the cemetery and on the other there were dwellings. A flag staff with the tricolor floating and a water trough completed the civic adornments.

Each company was provided with a mess hall but this was the last place we met up with this luxury until our return to the coast many months later. Besides one really had no use for a mess hall when the need was measured by the food provided. Consequently, the mess hall served mainly as a study hall when the rain prevented us from carrying out the regular drill schedule.

Promptly after arriving the drill began and we were informed that this would be the final touch before taking over a sector and that no trifling would be tolerated from anyone.

Machine gun work, gas drill, signal work all were pushed to the utmost during our stay of nine days.

The second day after our arrival we received our first mail and it certainly was a happy event. Everyone received at least one letter and many as many as half a dozen. Promptly everyone made a rush for letter paper and the village store was beseiged with trade.

While here many changes were made in the arrangement of the company and the formation adopted held during most of our stay in Europe with only the changes made necessary by circumstances.

A machine gun range was secured a few kilos out of town and this work was resumed. The forty-eight guns of the battalion were kept hot most of the time.

Between times, while we were resting, the streets must needs be cleaned and the battalion certainly proved themselves adepts as "white wing" artists. Some of the old timers of the village regarded this as almost as much of a calamity as the war but American sanitary measures won in the end.

The Community Washhouse

Here we met up with the French public washhouse where the dames of the village meet to discuss their neighbors' business and pound the dirt out of the family wash at the same time. Usually the washhouse is built over a stream and the washing process is carried out in vast stone vats. A wooden paddle and plenty of arm movement takes the place of soap and the clothes are dipped into the trough from time to time. The hammering is done on the stone edge of the pool and a wash board is unknown. A circle of village women can certainly make the dirt and gossip fly at the same time as they gather round the common pool on wash day.

To the Foothills of the Vosges

Toward dusk Wednesday, July 24, the battalion moved out of Sauville in the direction of the railroad and after a hike of some twelve kilometers or more brought up at the little town of Beuvannes, passing through Damblain and following the track most of the way.

Without ceremony or delay, we were packed into box cars, about fifty to a car, a French official came along and threw a little canned goods into each one much after the fashion one throws a bone to a strange dog, a jerky little engine backed up and hooked on and we were off.

The comfort to be derived from such a situation can be imagined. Everyone was overheated from the stiff hike, the night was cool and the available space for sleeping was less than a little.

During the night's ride we passed through the cities of Toul, Nancy and Luneville and at daybreak found ourselves at a little way-side station labeled Einvaux.

In an incredibly short time, the battalion detrained and was formed up on the road. Without even a suggestion as to when and where we might secure the morning meal, we were put under motion in the direction of one of the nearby mountain roads for we were now in the foothills of the Vosges.

The first thing of interest to come under our notice was a huge ammunition dump a kilo or so from the station. There were piles and heaps of shell of every calibre from the seventy-five to the largest in use. At first sight, one could mistake this for the chief munition depot of the western front but later we found that it was only a secondary dump and a small one at that.

Another sign of the growing nearness of the front came in the form of an order to form two columns, one on each side of the road, and under no circumstances were we to bunch up. A distance of five paces was to be maintained between individuals at all times. It was explained that this was a necessary troop movement and that it must be carried on in daylight and these precautions were taken to prevent the movement from being reported by the enemy air craft whose presence might be expected at any time.

Chasing the "Sausage"
Published Monday, May 12, 1919

As we climbed the steady rise above the station at Einvaux an observation balloon rose in the distance and to the untrained eyes appeared to be about five miles away.

Hiking steadily until noon it seemed as if we had circled that same O.B. (Observation Balloon) a dozen times and when we finally rushed into a small village off the main road for water and a chance at our reserve rations it was as far away as ever. After "killing our Willie" with a relish, we were allowed a few minutes to remove our shoes and look at the remains of our feet. Truly they were a sight to behold but the day was young yet at noon, and many miles before us so it was quite useless to make an attempt to do any repairing.

Taking to the road once more we resumed the chase of the elusive balloon and it is a certainty that our particular outfit will never forget the Vosges mountains or the tortuous stone roads winding over them. As night drew on men began to fall by the wayside either too tired or too footsore to proceed further. The farther we went the thinner the ranks became.

Along the way were many evidences of the struggle here in the early days of 1914. Wire obstructions, partially destroyed villages, once live machine gun pits, bits of trenches and the like gave evidence of the confidence of the French that the Huns would make their big attempt here instead of in the North and showed that there had been bitter fighting even in this locality.

Fontenoy-Le-Jute

About six o'clock of the evening of Friday, July 25, what remained of the little band arrived at Fontenoy-le-Jute. Of a battalion or over 700 men, about fifty were in at the finish.

Some little time was spent in figuring out if this really was our town and then we limped up the side of a hill into the town proper to our billets.

We had covered a little better than twenty-six miles under heavy marching and were practically green troops at that.

But the excitement of the day was not over by far. At eleven o'clock, we were served a meal consisting of hot "Wille," stewed tomatoes, bread and coffee and it certainly met with a hearty reception. It was the first square meal we had encountered for some time and our efforts at stowing it away showed.

While we were enjoying the unusually good meal Fritzie undertook to put on a little side show for our benefit and the benefit of the munitions dump at the nearby railroad of Azarailless.

The show went something like this. An enemy bombing plane attempted to kick off an egg (drop a bomb) on the ammunitions dump near the city. There chanced to be a full moon that night and the anti-aircraft guns were able to spot the offender easily. In a moment, almost, they had hemmed the raider in with a barrage of explosive shells and finally he flew directly into the moon. This afforded us a perfect view of the spectacle and gave the gunners every opportunity, but the Boche finally squirmed out and headed for his own lines but not before he had used his machine gun to good effect and killed and wounded several citizens in the nearby city of Baccarat.

During our stay in Fontenoy we found that these raids were a nightly occurrance and at the first sound of enemy avions we were out of our several lofts and stables and into the open either to see the fun or take to our heels as the occasion warranted.

We remained in Fontenoy eight days and the time was largely spent in one or another drill. Range work with the guns proved to be interesting because they took them out into the open and blazed away at most anything for a target. Here also we were taught the throwing of live grenades, hiking to a distant hilltop for that purpose one rainy Sabbath morning.

Mules and Money

Stable Sergeant Lewis Blieu drew his issue of mules and carts with full equipment and a mule train was a part of our forces from this point on.

We drew our first over seas pay here and encountered the money of the Republic of France for the first time in any amount. The French currency hadn't the crisp appearance of the good old greenback of our boyhood and was treated accordingly.

In addition to the thrills furnished by the air pirates, by climbing to the top of any of the nearby hills one could look toward the Nancy and Toul fronts and see the smoke of the battle line while at daybreak and the rumble of guns foretold a raid on some salient of the quiet front.

The next to the last day of our stay, the orders came in that we were to take over a section of the front and that the platoon sergeants and corporals of the gun squads were to accompany the Company commanders to the sector to be occupied and that two days later we were to follow in force and receive our try out at the trench warfare game.

The day following the departure of the noncommissioned officers was spent making ready for our own advent into the lines.

Vaxainville Taken Over

At dusk the night of August 3rd the battalion was again under way moving toward an unknown sector. The companies were formed up in combat order with the squads marching along side their respective gun and ammunition carts.

Our way was through the city of Azarailless and the towns of Gelacourt and Brouville. At the latter place the other companies moved off to different parts of the sector while we kept on in the direction of Vaxainville. When within a kilometer of this place we were halted and cautioned to maintain absolute silence as the front was not far distant.

As each platoon pulled into Vaxainville the platoon commander was joined by a guide from the organization then occupying the salient and led forward to the positions to be occupied.

While the gun positions were being taken over, Lieutenant C. J. Rew relieved the machine gun commander at Vaxainville and established company headquarters there. The Headquarters Platoon remained in the town with the company commander.

The story of the relief put on by the First Platoon is the story of the company on that night for the method was the same as in the other platoons, the locality being the sole difference.

Keeping on through Vaxainville the gun platoons crossed the bridge below and at the forks of the road just ahead came the parting of the ways. The Third Platoon took the road to the left in the direction of Pettonville and took over the positions directly ahead of that place. The Second Platoon followed the road to the right and advanced to the "pill box" on the road parallel to the front and well ahead of the other platoons and took over these points with the cement fortification as a center point of defense.

The First Platoon advanced over the road the second had taken but only for about a kilometer.

Suddenly from up ahead came the terse command to halt and upon advancing, the information that it was the relief approaching, we were allowed to advance. Our challengers proved to be the commander of the old platoon and his runner, and the guides were immediately set to the task of leading the squads to the different emplacements. Meanwhile the officers and platoon runners proceeded to the headquarters some six hundred meters across an open field and into the edge of the woods.

The sergeants and runners were quartered in one room of a large dugout while the nearby gun squad occupied the other room. The officer in charge chose a shell-proof of "elephant iron" for his quarters.

As each gun was relieved and the old crew had started for the rear the corporal reported to the officer and then the platoon report was carried to the company commander at Vaxainville to be phoned in to the battalion and on up.

Trench Life
Published Monday, May 19, 1919

Some idea of the regular routine of trench life as we found it in this quiet sector of Alsace can be gained from the orders we were called upon to carry out daily.

At dusk and dawn came the "stand to" hours. The exact time differed with the season of the year and was changed accordingly. At "stand to" each gun squad was at its place, guns and ammunition were inspected and everything possible was done to anticipate an attack for these were the hours when raids were carried out and the great attacks were launched.

During a gas alarm the order of the regular "stand to" was observed for it was the ordinary thing for the Germans to "come over" under the cover of the gas barrage.

The only lights permissible were those in the dugouts and these must be carefully covered.

The time honored countersign was in use, and furnished a touch of the romance of wars of other days. The counter-sign and parole came in by wire at noon each day and was carried by runners to the platoons and by other runners to the gun squads.

Invariably, the infantry sentries and patrols would have one pronunciation for the strange foreign words used and the machine gunners another and the mixups were often very funny.

An Enemy Surprise

The following account of a happening of the first day in the trenches is very much the story of our first ten days there or what might be termed our period of service in the second line of defense.

"Those members of the Company composing the Headquarters Platoon and those of the First Platoon stationed in the vicinity of platoon headquarters, received their baptism of fire about mid-day August 4, the day following their advent there.

"A carrying party made up of Headquarters men, under the command of Corporal Ivan Shanafelt, Signal Corporal, had been detailed by the company commander, Lieutenant C. J. Rew, to carry forward rations for the noon meal to the men in the trenches. The party left Vaxainville encumbered with containers of food and proceeded up the open road in the direction of the second line, ignorant of the covered road generally used for this purpose and advisable for the use of parties of more than two men during the daylight hours. The presence of Jerry's 'sausage' the ever present observation balloon, hovering over the German town of Domevre, had also been forgotten by all.

"The trip was without incident until Corporal Shanafelt had gained the shelter of the woods and was within sight of the sheltering dugout occupied by Platoon Headquarters. The platoon sergeants, headquarters men and those of the squad stationed nearby were lined up in anticipation of the approaching mess. Suddenly from over the Boche lines came a weird sound, as of an approaching hurricane. Louder and louder it shrieked, drawing closer with the speed of an express train.

"At the first sound one of the sergeants and the corporal of the nearby squad looked at each other and simultaneously fell on their faces in the shelter of the dugout. The others of the party remained fixed in various attitudes, all as if paralyzed by the strange occurrence.

"With a final shriek the shell was upon them, exploding some twenty-five yards behind their position. The watchful balloon had informed a waiting battery of the stir behind our lines and this was their reply.

"The shelling continued until Jerry had placed an even dozen in that particular locality, but a change had come over the 'trench rookies'—they had taken cover alongside their wiser companions."

Stirring Air Battles

During these ten days 'up' at Vaxainville we witnessed many stirring air battles for the weather was clear a part of the time and the amount of air activities was considerable.

Both the enemy planes and our own sought to direct their respective batteries of artillery and this alone was the cause of many sharp contests.

A battery of anti-aircraft seventy-fives, or as the Tommys call them, 'Archies,' was located on the hilltop between Vaxainville and Pettonville and they broke loose at the first sight of the enemy avions.

When one stops to think that an allowance of 10,000 rounds is made to each of these guns to wing a single plane and that even if this number of shells must be extended to bring down a plane the investment is a profitable one, and idea of the firing done daily can be gained. However, the French average is a plane for each 3,000 shells and often they surpass this record.

A common sight was to see fleets of twenty or thirty bombing planes speeding toward Matz, Essen or the Rhine towns bent on carrying on the war from within. Hours later these same aerial armadas would return less a half dozen or so of the trim birds as the price of the expedition.

The Prussian Guard

This same Baccarat sector showed many signs of the early days of the struggle. Everywhere extended the network of trenches, dugouts and emplacements constructed to hold this southern part of the line after the Huns had made their initial dash in the fall of 1914 and which had given the allies little or no trouble and had come to be a sort of finishing school in the fine points of war.

Not only were the American divisions given their tryout here but the Imperial troops were brought into this salient for training and after certain divisions had been worn down on the more active sectors to the north they were brought down here for rest. At the time of our entry into this sector the Austrians were holding the other side of the line but as our time grew to a close a number of the famous Prussian Guard regiments were brought in and at one time the rumors were current that an offensive might be attempted here and that our vigilance would have to be doubled.

Although we were unaware of any connection at the time, the Ohio division was destined to meet these same crack troops at several points on the Western front and it is with pride that the 37th can point to the fact that never were they at a disadvantage in dealing with the best the Kaiser's army afforded.

In the Front Line

The night of Tuesday, August 13, the Company was relieved in the B positions by Company D, 136th M. B. Battalion, and in turn relieved the infantry machine gun company holding the front line of defense in and around the village of Migneville.

One relief is much like another. There is always the same hope that the night will remain cloudy and that the enemy will see fit not to stage an artillery show at the wrong moment.

Company headquarters was established at Migneville with the First Platoon located just ahead of the town. The Third Platoon occupied positions in and around the town of Herbevilliers. The low range of hills between and ahead of these towns was held by the Second Platoon.

The same method of rationing was used here as in Vaxainville with the important difference that food was more plentiful and that the positions were so located that the carrying parties had little difficulty in getting it up.

Perhaps the most interesting event of our stay there was the night raid in which the Boche avion attempted to bomb the headquarters at Migneville and succeeded in blowing up the remains of the village church within three hundred yards of the troop quarters.

Aerial activity of all kinds was carried on over the line continually.

About the third or fourth day there was a French flyer who brought down his opponent nearby and most of the Hun craft was carried off for trophies by the infantrymen stationed in the locality.

The Gas Barrage

On the night of August 17, the thirtieth U.S. Engineers launched a gas attack near Herbevillier.

The attack was carried out by means of trench mortars placed in the front line and was intended as a complete surprise to the Germans.

Promptly at midnight the barrage opened on the left of the line and spread slowly to the right. The infantry units and the machine gun support had been previously notified to 'stand to' and be on the alert for an enemy move.

At Herbevillier the American front joined with the French sector on the North and while the American barrage was at its height, a raiding party of French 'went over' and took six prisoners.

Our Third Platoon was stationed in and to the left of Herbevillier and were under the command of Second Lieutenant John K. North. They had received the general order to 'stand to' and had made all preparations to receive the Boche in case he essayed to test their strength.

About the regular 'stand to' hour (near dawn) the enemy artillery opened up and under cover of their barrage the German machine gunners and infantry made an attack on the French and American positions. During the scrimmage the French suffered a loss of eight prisoners and the Americans their tempers because existing fire orders had prevented them from taking an active part in the fight.

The German guns dropped close to a thousand shells in the vicinity of the town and during this Lieutenant North and Sergeant Carl Hentz were busy going from one gun emplacement to another. On one of their trips, a shell registered almost a direct hit on them, tearing a gap in a nearby stone wall and burying them under pulverized stone and debris. The lieutenant and Sergeant Hentz took cover in a barbed wire entanglement and were badly raked as a result.

Damaging Domevre

Captain K. T. Siddall was battalion commander during this period and on one occasion made the Huns of our particular locality rather uncomfortable. The observer of our old friends, the 'sausage balloon' at Brouville, had reported to him that there seemed to be too much activity behind the enemy lines and that on a certain night they would be working on a bridge in the general direction of the town of Do-mevre.

Accordingly, the captain gathered his firing data and rushed up to the Second Platoon location. Moving one of the guns forward a safe distance to conceal the position he opened up a barrage on the locality of the bridge. The merry song of the Vickers broke in on the construction work and the next morning the friendly observer reported, that to the captain's credit, the enemy working party had been thoroughly routed with several stretcher cases.

Leaving Megneville the night of August 23, we proceeded to the town of Mervillier where we were put through the 'delouser' on the suspicion we might have acquired 'cooties' during our tour of duty in the trenches.

The night following we hiked the remainder of the way into Gelacourt where we were put into the so called rest camp.

The week following was spent getting as much rest as possible between fits of drill.

Guarding the O. B.

While the company was at the rest camp, the first section of the First Platoon was detailed to the neighboring village of Brouville for anti-avion duty near the American observation balloon. This was our old friend, the sausage, we had followed so long.

Although the element of danger was lacking in this assignment, the excitement of keeping enemy airplanes away from the all important sausage more than compensated.

The section was under the command of Sergeant Chester Keyes and was made up of squads in charge of Corporals Demmler and Damicon. The first squad was stationed on the crest of a hill overlooking the village of Reherry and looking toward the front lines. Corporal Demmler's gun was placed just outside the village in an open space in the center of a plum orchard.

During their stay there, two attempts were made to burn the balloon. On one occasion, a single plane made the attempt and was frightened off by the combined fire of the anti-aircraft seventy-fives, near Vaxainville, and the machine guns.

A second attempt was made the day before they were relieved. A number of planes appeared over the American lines and seemed to be engaged in combat among themselves. The anit-aircraft guns failed to fire upon them, fearing to hit our own planes. All at once a single plane detached itself from the group and darted toward Brouville and the Observation Balloon. The machine gunner on the hill seeing the error of the A. A. guns opened fire. This was the signal to the other squad and in a moment a concentrated fire was opened from all quarters on the Boche.

Corporal Demmler's gun did especially deadly work, placing a belt at close range. Finding the locality too warm the enemy pilot wheeled his machine and took flight in the direction of his own lines, falling a few meters inside the German territory.

Amateur Theatricals
Published Monday, May 26, 1919

All was not work at the Gelacourt barracks, for the show put on by the talent of the company stands out as one of the most pleasant events of our time in France.

The performance was given at the YMCA tent under the auspices of the two women representatives and was under the personal direction of Grant A. Martin, former Pittsburgh actor/manager.

Others of the cast were Private Frank Murray of Pittsburgh, composer of ragtime hits and vocalist; Sergeant Kennerdell George of Kent; Privates Clair Dunning, (K.I.A.) and Ezra Creese, Ravenna; Private Theron McCay, Coshocton, while Musician George P. Fleishman, Ravenna, featured with a cornet solo.

A popular program of song and dialogue was given, with piano selections by Murray and McCay.

The 'Y' tent was packed to overflowing and a more enthusiastic audience of 'first-nighters' never greeted any production anywhere.

Thirteen Days Up

Again on the night of September 1, we moved toward the front and into the "B" positions around Vaxainville and Pettonville. The relief was much the same as on the former occasions and was carried out without a single happening of more than ordinary interest.

This second time up covered a period of thirteen days. The normal time was ten days, but as we were about to move into the Migneville line, orders came holding us in the second line for another ten days.

A considerable unrest was noticeable on the part of the German artillery, for where they had maintained a regular program of shelling during our previous stay, they now opened up on us at the most unexpected moments.

The towns of Reherry and Vaxainville were shelled frequently, while both the first and second lines were under fire at some point continually. An attack on the part of the Boche was expected nightly and the alarms were frequent. Kicking the gun crews out at all hours became a habit and long watches at the guns became the rule rather than the exception.

During this same period, orders came from higher up that the plan of defense must be changed, and new emplacements for each of the guns must be located and constructed. This work was carried out under the direction of Captain Siddall. All of it had to be done at night and every care taken that marks of fresh digging were not in evidence when the German "sausages" went up in the morning. To add to the discomforts of the situation, it rained almost night and day. The gun squads had been forced to make many changes in their sleeping quarters and some of them found themselves without a home at all. Also some of the dugouts they were forced to occupy were filled with water and spending a dry night was worse that impossible.

The enemy artillery took advantage of the rainy weather and placed as many gas shells as possible around us. The odor of gas hung heavy in the bushes and care was necessary to prevent kicking up the stuff.

Consequently, it was with a feeling of relief that we received the order to pack up and meet the relief on the night of September 14 and clear the sector for good.

Our tour of duty in the salient had extended over a period of forty-two days in service in the second, first and third lines of defense.

The several platoons assembled at Vaxainville and after the 95th French Machine Gun Company had been guided in, the start was made for an indefinite place to the rear.

Northward Bound

The small hours of the morning found us billeted in the village of Menarmont near the RAF bombing center.

Our four day stay was largely spent in drawing a little new equipment and in watching the maneuvers of the huge bombing machines. Many of the officers and a few of men were fortunate enough to be taken for a flight by the polite Britishers in charge.

On September 18, the company was divided into platoons and went to different rail centers to load. The Third and First loaded at Gerberville.

The same platoons detrained at Longeville the day following and the entire battalion assembled at Fains, near the city of Bar-le-Duc. After a day here the men were loaded into French motor camions and started for the front while the wagon and mule trains proceeded later over the same route.

Each squad carried its own gun and equipment and some ammunition. From these precautions, it was easy to determine that we were not going anywhere for a weekend party but just where we were bound for was a mystery.

After an all night ride over roads that were anything but smooth, we were put off six miles back of the front and told that it would be a foot proposition from there on.

The Verdun Front

From the sign boards along the way, we had determined that we were in the locality of Verdun and going into a very lively part of the battle line. As we climbed out of the trucks the star shells and Very lights illuminated the surrounding country. The whistle of an approaching H.E. shell (high-explosive) helped strengthen this impression.

The six miles up to where we were to take cover in the forest were endless and the weight of the equipment and guns made the hike ten times as long. Just what it meant to carry these burdens cannot be told here or anywhere for it was a terrible drag on each man.

The way was uphill and down and the roads were stony and rough. At length, we came to the remains of the town of Recicourt and after climbing another immense hill crossed the highway and settled in the edge of the forest to await the dawn.

We were now in the famed Argonne forest in the section known as Hesse Woods and were in reserve in what was termed the Avocourt Sector for that town or rather the remains of that town were just ahead a few kilometers.

Of course, our kitchen and supplies were detained on the road and foodless days were the rule. Blackberries were plentiful and these helped out a lot in the food famine. The trains came up, however, on the 24th and we had a slender meal or two then.

Intensive Battle Preparation

During the five days we remained in the woods we saw much of the preparations for the big battle to be opened up. Guns and more guns were hauled forward, cannon of every size and use. Naval rifles up to sixteen inches, anti-aircraft guns on motor trucks, trench mortars of a dozen makes, howitzers, field guns, heavy and light, were drawn up for the heavy barrage to come.

Aerial activity was immense. Enemy and friendly planes met and battled overhead at all hours while the anti-aircraft guns barked endlessly from both lines.

The chief American artillery support was furnished by the 128th Light Field Artillery from the Pennsylvania Guard division. These gunners worked day and night preparing for the big show and their seventy-fives were chained hub-to-hub with endless rounds of shells when the morning of the offense arrived.

This outfit had operated in the St. Mihiel offensive only a few days before and the men and horses were nearly exhausted but their efforts were untiring, notwithstanding the hardship under which they labored.

A Glimpse of General Pershing

Just before dusk Thursday, September 15, we moved forward once more taking with us the mule train and kitchen.

On our way, we were caught in a traffic jam and the automobile of the Commanding General of the American Expeditionary Forces, John J. Pershing, stopped in the midst of our train for several minutes. Later that night, the General rode up to a headquarters near our location and we glimpsed him again.

The closer the front we came the deeper the mud and the last mile before the place where we were to have supper was knee-deep.

Drawing up behind a considerable hill we were instructed to do away with our blanket rolls, extra clothing and the like and carry very little in addition to our reserve rations. This excess baggage was made into rolls and carried to a salvage dump a mile distant.

The guns, equipment, and as much ammunition as could be carried with us was removed from carts and they were sent back of the barrage zone to follow us as soon as the drive had been commenced.

All these preparations finished, a supper of beans and corned beef was served and finding a place to sit in the darkness was impossible. At ten o'clock the order was given to pick up the equipment and move on.

The way was up the slope of the hill that had seemed to afford us protection from the line. After following a walk of duck boards for some time we emerged into a sort of park. Apparently, it had been part of a considerable estate before the rival armies had made the Argonne forest a playground for the rough guns of war.

The Barrage Opens

At length, the company halted on the forward slope of the hill and the captain passed the word back that the barrage would start shortly and that we were not to be alarmed for the shells would be going over, at least for the first few hours anyway.

A little after eleven o'clock, a battery of seventy-fives opened up from the hill behind us. Soon a battery on our left spoke up. Shortly fifty or sixty guns were in action. Now and then the dull boom of a big gun could be heard under the sharp crack of the smaller pieces. These shells were going over to disturb the Huns in the back areas.

By one o'clock, the barrage was on in full strength. Everywhere came flashes betraying the presence of a gun. Great streaks of fire followed the shells a hundred feet or more on their way.

A dull boom now and then and an unusually bright flash gave proof that it was anything but a one-sided fight for the Boche artillery was getting in its work along with our own.

About this time we moved up over duck boards into a kind of swamp. Captain Siddall selected a covered position and instructed that all should get as much rest as possible. Sleep came easily in spite of the awful racket of the guns and it was a sleepy crowd that he routed out just before daybreak for the big start off.

Over the Top

Moving out in the general direction of the highway, we had left some hours before we wound through the undergrowth for some distance finally striking the road. Here we met the mule train of some National Army regimental machine gun company. The outfit was hopelessly lost and was more so an hour later.

Our task was to follow down a series of duck boards and into the trench system and eventually 'over the top' at a distant P.P.

Had it worked out as planned, all would have been well but the infantry mussed things up with the result that our company doubled back and forth some fifty times between the road and the first of the trenches. Meanwhile, the enemy guns had become active on all sides.

About the twenty-fifth trip the company lost heart and sat down in the ditch to think it over. With a ripping crash, a high explosive shell fell in the midst of the mule train on the road and scattered pieces of man, mule and cart in all directions. It had been about a ten-inch and was the spur needed to revive our lagging ambition.

Finally, we were given a clear way through the trenches and at length found ourselves in the front line. An orderly came back with the instruction that Sergeant Keys was to scale the parapet at that point with his section of two guns. The movement was carried out and meantime the remainder of the company moved off.

Finding ourselves lost, we set out in the direction we supposed they had gone and met the platoon commander, Lieutenant Rew, who had become alarmed and returned to locate us.

No Man's Land

Following the line of advance closely, we came out into what had been 'no man's land' for four years. The earth had been churned by the shell fire to a depth of ten feet or more and there was shell hole in shell hole.

Next we came to the enemy line. Our artillery had done their work here as well. The pill boxes and emplacements were ruined and even the deep dugouts were in many cases caved in.

An hour's advance brought us up with Captain Siddall and the others of the company. Here, we saw our first killed and first wounded American, the first the victim of a Hun bayonet and the second a grenade. Also we met a number of prisoners on their way back under infantry guard.

Everywhere were dugouts, trenches, machine gun nests, wire, and all the evidence of the four years of constant battle.

Just after noon we were met by the mule train and late in the afternoon halted for rest and food.

A word of explanation is necessary here. C and D Companies of the battalion were in the second wave, that is the reserve wave, and were supporting the 147th Infantry. This accounts for the apparent lack of action on our part. By noon of the second day, the reserve was abreast of the first wave and so it remained the remainder of the time up.

Moving forward the train and company separated again, the train following the road and the company cutting down through the forest.

Dusk found us united again and making ready to spend the night on the first rise of the bloody hilltop overlooked by the famed city of Montfaucon.

Four Hun "Souvenirs"
Monday, June 2, 1919

By Charles M. Conaway

While many German prisoners were taken by the different organizations during the several offensives, to Private Keeter and Private Sam Lafalce belongs the credit for capturing four 'Heines' behind our lines several hours after the first wave had swept by.

It was the first day of the Meuse-Argonne drive and we were nearing our advance objective for that day when the company was halted for rest near the far edge of the great Argonne forest. Immediately, small parties began to detach themselves and go through the several abandoned dugouts in the vicinity in search of souvenirs.

Keeter and Lefalce in the course of their search came upon one shelter deeper than the rest and before investigating further called down the stairs in German for the occupants to come up and surrender. To their surprise, four little round caps showed themselves immediately and they found themselves in the role of captor with four Germans of tender age on their hands. The prisoners, ranging in age from fourteen to eighteen years, kept begging the Americans not to kill them and not to cut off their noses and ears (as they explained later they had been told by the officers would be the case if they allowed themselves to be taken prisoner by the Americans), mixing gutteral German with bursts of tears.

Keeter reassured his prisoners by telling them that he would take them to the proper authorities and protect them from being shot as snipers. After giving the Company a good look at his 'find,' he marched them off in search of someone in authority to turn them over to.

On Dead Man's Hill

The following morning the company moved forward, in accordance with orders, in support of the Second Battalion, 148th Infantry, toward the village of Iviory, the Divisional objective.

The company was formed into battle order, in columns of platoons with the Headquarters leading and the First, Second and Third following in regular order. The first obstacle encountered was a wire entanglement through which a gap was cut by the runners large enough to allow the passing through in single file.

Advancing through a narrow valley, we crossed the rise where the Germans had met the attack of the gallant French, at a former time, when the Huns had been directed by the Crown Prince in person from the famous tower at Monfaucon. Evidences of the earlier struggle were furnished by the deep trenches, the numerous wire entanglements and the shell-torn landscape.

Following in the wake of the assaulting infantry, we advanced down the slope on the right of the village. It was here that we encountered our first taste of machine gun and rifle fire. The enemy fire was directed from a clump of bushes on our right and from the tower of the church on our left. Here, we suffered our first causality, Private John Lackey getting a bullet in the leg while his platoon was taking cover. He was carried to an old trench by Lieutenant C. J. Rew, his platoon commander, and left there in a place of safety until medical attention arrived.

During the entire action Captain Siddall was far in the lead, closely followed by Lieutenant Harold Hubbell, reconnaissance officer, and the Headquarters platoon. They were first to charge the opposite slope and when the other platoons came up the Captain gave orders to 'keep down' for the enemy was putting over a machine gun barrage.

About this time, the Boche artillery opened up on the village and vicinity, throwing over gas shells at regular intervals. A number of gas casualties among the infantry was the result.

Beyond Iviory

Our farthest gain for that day was made when the company was ordered toward the crest of the hill in the direction of a small orchard. The platoons were ordered to take cover and keep down while the First Section of the First Platoon went forward to the crest of the hill and mounted their guns. Captain Siddall led the section and prepared to put over a barrage to cover the advancing infantry.

Before the gunners could carry out their fire orders, a runner appeared with a message for the infantry commander to the effect that the enemy was counter attacking in large numbers and a retreat was advisable. At once, the infantry began to withdraw and the machine gun company was called upon to perform its function as a rearguard body for the covering of the retreat of the rifle men.

The First Platoon, under Lieutenant Rew, was ordered to 'mount gun' and cover the withdrawal. The guns were mounted under the cover of a ruined dugout system along a sunken road and laid on the crest of the hill in anticipation of the waves of German infantry previously reported.

Before the fire orders could be carried out, a runner came up with an order for Lieutenant Rew to fall back. This was carried out a squad at a time and without the loss of a man. The maneuver taking place under a continuous fire from the enemy guns.

Desperate Battling

About halfway up the next slope, the guns of the company were ordered into action. The First Platoon setting up behind the cover of several piles of barbed wire in rolls, along a dinky railroad track, and the Second Platoon in one of the old trenches. The Third Platoon had become detached in the excitement and had continued the retreat, wandering to the left of the village.

In the meantime, the infantry had re-formed their lines and were making all preparations to meet the enemy when they came over. For a period of perhaps an hour there was a lull, with the enemy digging in on the hill we had so recently vacated.

Then the battle opened! The Germans opened up with the concentrated fire of artillery, trench mortars, one-pounders and machine guns. The several machine gun companies replied from our side of the hill, supported by the infantry fire.

The enemy fire grew so hot that the company was forced to withdraw still further and they finally dug in on the same hill they had advanced from that morning. At the same time the infantry regiments and the other machine gun units also retired.

Following our retirement, we dug in, completing a set of partially dug infantry trenches and mounting the guns a hundred yards forward in anticipation of further advances by the Huns.

Towards evening, the Third Platoon rejoined us and we rested through the night in preparation for another attempt the next day.

Our Ammunition Train

Second Lieutenant Sam A. Miller and the men serving under him as drivers and guides for the company ammunition train during the great Meuse-Argonne offensive are due great credit for their work in bringing up the ammunition reserve and during the time the company was in the lines.

When the company went over the top in the grey of the morning of September 26, the train was following as close behind as possible under existing conditions, and when the company halted for rest and rations toward evening of the first day they were joined by them. Lieutenant Miller had led his men and mules over the road hastily improvised by the engineer forces and up to the combat forces with scarcely a delay in spite of the havoc wrought by the artillery of both sides.

During the advance of the second day, the train was at no time more than a kilometer in the rear of the company, and at the hour of the great resistance around and beyond the village of Iviory the train was brought up to within less than one hundred meters of the forward machine gun positions and on a line with the infantry front line. Different machine gun companies were supplied with sorely needed ammunition at this time as well as a part of the infantry.

During this action, the entire train was under heavy artillery and machine gun fire, while snipers sought to cripple their advance by firing at the officer in charge and his guides.

On to Cierges

The morning of the third day, a fresh start was made with a well-arranged plan of attack. Each infantry unit was supported by a certain machine gun unit and this formation was maintained as closely as possible throughout the drive.

As we went forward, the enemy artillery opened up point blank on the surrounding hilltops and actually blasted them off in the faces of the advancing troops.

The hill upon which we had operated the day before was a veritable inferno and it seemed that no living thing could exist there. But the advance kept on and its regularity proceeded with the smoothness of a finished machine.

Our artillery support at this time consisted of four captured German seventy-sevens and a small store of captured ammunition. Even the desultory fire from these pieces sounded good to our tortured ears as contrasted from the thousands of shells hurled over by the enemy.

The objective for the day was the enemy town of Cierges. The Company reached the locality by noon and toward mid-afternoon the assault was organized and begun.

The infantry advanced in waves under the fire of the machine guns and as a wave was mowed down another sprang up to take its place. The enemy made use of machine guns and trench mortars and poured a continuous and withering fire into the assaulting ranks.

Again and again, the ever thinning ranks were formed up. Each time to be cut to pieces and the few survivors banded together for another attempt.

Our Company was in the thickest of the battle and Ravenna gunners poured a hot fire into the ranks of the Hun infantry as they formed above the town the celebrated mass formation in an attempt to counterattack. At the same time they cleaned out enemy snipers and machine gun nests without number.

Failure of the Tanks

Night of the third day found the company dug in where the attack had been started. The infantry had been cut to pieces and had called for help after taking Montfaucon the second day. The artillery had not succeeded in coming up and the situation was to say the least critical.

This same night word came up that the French Whippet tanks were coming up and that at daybreak they would crack the nut at Cierges where the infantry had failed.

Sure enough, the morning of the fourth day thirteen of the marvels put in their appearance. The infantry formed up to follow and hold the advantage gained.

No more had the assault been sighted by the Boche artillery than they opened up with every available gun. The tanks proceeded for a short way, the drivers became discouraged and opening the safety door, beat a hasty retreat. This left the infantry in a sorrier plight than even the day before and the story of their end is the same as in the former attempt.

The remainder of the stay in this hot and none too comfortable position was largely a repetition of the first days. Endless attempts were made to carry the town and several succeeded but before the infantry could secure a firm footing the enemy artillery would make the town and environs too hot for anything to live in.

Our Company was ahead of the infantry in most of these attacks and the small percentage of losses is nothing short of a miracle.

The Cost of Battle
Monday, June 9, 1919
by Charles M. Conaway

The casualty list stood as follows at the time we withdrew, October 2, Claude Davis, Kent, shrapnel in arm; Wilbur Minnich, Ravenna, accident; Wallace Tinder, Pittsburgh, shrapnel in leg; William Myers, Kent, timed shrapnel in leg; John Lackey, Hamilton, bullet in leg;

Hubert Strayer, Kent, bullet in head; James Ryan, Philadelphia, shrapnel in arm; Lieutenant Hubbell, bullet in thigh; Captain Siddall, mustard gassed; Raymond Hill, shrapnel in back; Charles McMullen, Ashland, Kentucky, bullet in shoulder; Berger Jacobsen, Ravenna, shrapnel in chest; Raymond Bath, Cincinnati, bullet in chest; George Fleishman, Ravenna, mustard gassed; Victor Sodaker, Coshocton, mustard gassed; Lee M. Gray, gassed; Thomas E. Jones, shell-shocked.

Back to Recicourt

The last two days of the drive brought relief for one outfit and another on all sides of C Company. Repeated assurances came up from battalion headquarters that a company from the new division was on its way. Finally, as the casualty was growing alarming and the food and water situation was hopeless, Lieutenant Rew, who had assumed command after Captain Siddall's misfortune, decided to withdraw.

The forenoon of October 2, the company drew back over the ground so hotly contested the week previous and connecting with the mule train made their way toward Recicourt and Hesse Woods.

The Ravenna company was the last of the Ohio division to leave the line and at the time of the withdrawal was entirely surrounded by the troops of other divisions. Had the company commander not adopted the course he did, doubtless we would have been holding the line of the Meuse yet.

Leaving Recicourt, the trip to Choloy was made in camions, while the train followed later.

After three days at Choloy, we hiked to Foug where we were to take trucks for Pannes in the St. Mihiel salient. It was about five kilometers to Foug and reaching there we were ordered to rest along the road and wait for the trucks. While we waited a fine rain set in. To top it all off, the trucks failed to take us as intended, the train had already gone on and we were stranded in this place while some outfit waited patiently to be relieved up in the lines.

At length, Lieutenant Rew commandeered the railway station and we moved in bag and baggage and occupied the place for two days or until the battalion commander saw fit to send for us.

Foug is a place of considerable size with important factories, most of them making shells at that time, and the number of people using the railway station was large. A great many of the inhabitants were employed in Toul and even in Paris and the confusion of their comings and goings through the 150 or so soldiers in the station can be imagined.

Of course, all this excitement was all right but the fact that the kitchen and rations had gone ahead with the train troubled us most. Everyone was dead broke for we had not had a pay for some months and with all kinds of food for sale in the shops we added two foodless days to Mr. Hoover's list. Besides we had scarcely eaten for three weeks before.

The St. Mihiel Salient

When the trucks finally came they took us to the village of Pannes and unloaded us in the dead of the night. Billets were secured in the loft of a barn that shell fire had almost wrecked but not so badly that it couldn't be used to house troops in. Also the kitchen got busy and put up a meal. Then we crawled up a rickety old ladder into our suite. When the fellows went to go down in the morning they marveled that the place hadn't collapsed during the night.

The next night we set out on foot with the train and after some twelve kilometers pulled into the woods near the Chateau of St. Benoit. Guides showed the way to the gun positions and kitchen location and the relief was reported complete in a short time.

St. Benoit is located midway between the cities of Thiacourt and Chambley. Mr. Irvin S. Cobb gives a very fine description of this locality in his article on the St. Mihiel drive in a recent number of the *Saturday Evening Post.* Mr. Cobb tells of the little town of Benney near where we were located.

The line we were called upon to hold here was the one established at the close of the St. Mihiel offensive, and in fact the 37th had relieved the troops who had put on the drive. Consequently this was what is termed a live front and compared with the trench sectors of the early years of the war.

Our Company held a salient surrounded on three sides by the enemy and consisted almost entirely of the woods. The first platoon held the front of the woods with the first section located just ahead of Louisville Farm and in plain sight and sniping distance of the enemy. The second section held the far corner of the woods and was within calling distance of the infantry P.P.s with the main strength of the infantry at our back. The second platoon held the front facing the Chateau and in support. Right up among them the third platoon held the third side.

Daily firing problems were worked out by Sergeant Carl Hentz under Lieutenant "Jim" Pease's direction. The Huns held a small town just ahead of the Third's positions and across a small lake. A barrage from their guns spoiled several attempts to bring up supplies and ammunition into this forward stronghold, by train. The success of this harassing fire was attested by the artillery observers posted nearby.

The favorite diversion of the enemy artillery in this locality was placing gas shells in the half mile square of woods we occupied. Heavy rains had preceded our entry and the woods were damp and the gas lingered everywhere. Movement in any direction was dangerous on that account for the deadly stuff was easily stirred up and the gas mask was found to be practically useless under conditions such as these.

Twin Enemies—Gas and Mud

Every night the infantry petty posts were treated to mustard gas and as high as twenty-one cripples were led away one morning while more than one unfortunate paid with his life.

The gas came in all varieties and the woods had an odor like a market house, after a night of 'strafing.'

Of course, the Boche gunners worked out with high explosive and shrapnel as well as gas and the infantry suffered heavily from this fire as well.

Boche avions were up all the time and it was necessary to keep under cover during the day to prevent the positions from being spotted and shelled out.

One-pounder cannon were used by both sides extensively. The enemy had the habit of drawing a pounder up into their forward positions after nightfall and making things generally uncomfortable for everyone in our immediate locality.

The greatest feature of the place was the deep, cozy, wet, uncomfortable MUD. The traces of roads were muddy. It was muddy in the forest. The open fields were regular seas of mud. It was with great difficulty that supplies were brought up and with greater difficulty that the heavy boxes of grenades, ammunition, and so on were carried over the mile and two mile distances to the isolated gun positions. The roads and paths through the woods were winding and it was necessary to go two miles to reach a place a half mile away.

Although so-called 'action' was lacking in the week spent here the days and nights were alike filled with endless work and movement; a great many of the company had been or were sick and no one was really well; consequently it was with joy that we were relieved by a regimental machine gun company from the Keystone division. This new outfit had made their way through from Chateau Thierry after an astounding number of days there. The company was entirely of new men, recently drafted, and the majority of whom had never seen a machine gun or heard the whistle of a shell.

Bound for Belgium

The morning of October 17, we hiked back to Pannes to join the train which had pulled back the night before. The guns were hauled back by truck.

During our wait for the trucks that were to speed us back to the neighborhood of Foug once more, the Salvation Army workers prepared a great quantity of hot chocolate for distribution to the company. The night was cold and this went far to make up for the supper we might have had.

The next morning, we found ourselves in the village of Dongermain. A railhead was located here and the speculation ran high as to which direction we would start when we were finally loaded and away.

Many favored the sunny clime of far-off Italy. A few ventured the opinion that we were to help out the British in the north. Even one of the more imaginative ones said we were going to Belgium, he felt sure.

Midnight, October 20, found the carts, wagons and animals loaded and the men climbing to their places in the box cars. Shortly after the train was underway and in a northerly direction.

Our way skirted the battlefront for a time, then through the environs of the city of Paris, over toward the coast and following the channel across the border of the kingdom of Belgium.

Wanton Destruction

We detrained at Woesten, Belgium, October 22 and pitched our tents in the early gray of the morning in the midst of what had been the third line of defense of the British armies for four years of trench fighting. The country about us was a picture of desolation and wanton destruction. The guns of the enemy had leveled the villages and torn up the roads. Trenches and dugouts were in evidence everywhere. Huge piles of forgotten shells marked where the British artillery had worked.

The next day, the start toward the then active front was made. The entire division moved as a body and for once the cover of darkness was disregarded and we started out in broad daylight.

As we advanced in the direction of what had been the city of Ypres real meaning of the four years of constant struggle came to us as it could only through actual observation of the work of the war demon.

The locations of once prosperous cities and beautiful villages were marked by signs erected by the French to the effect that 'Ici Ypres,' here is Ypres, and so on. Now and then, a twisted steel rail remained to mark where a well-placed shell had found the horse-car line or perhaps an iron pipe protruded at an odd angle just to remind one of the gas and water mains used here only a short four years before.

Miles and miles of barbed wire entanglements stretched out in every direction. Here and there a bit of camouflaging remained to mark where a battery had once thrown out its deadly rain of steel. The very earth was wrecked. Shell hole cut into shell hole and in places the ground had been churned to a depth of ten or twenty feet.

As we advanced, the trenches gave way to redoubts built up from the surface. The very fact that a hole will fill up while one digs in this locality made trenches of the ordinary kind quite useless. Consequently, earthworks and fortifications of concrete and sand bags took the places of trenches.

Pill boxes without number littered the landscape. Dwelling houses made of brick had been treated to an inner shell of some six or eight feet of concrete and artillery and machine guns installed therein. In time the brick had been blown away and the battered concrete alone remained. In the early accounts of the war one read much of the fighting at such and such a farm. The farmhouse would be fortified in this manner and became a regular stronghold.

The real cost of the war was apparent by the rows and patches of dull white crosses each marking the last resting place of a 'Tommy' or 'Heiney' depending on the side of the line. Some of these crosses bore helmets as reminders of the occupants. Here and there, a cross would lean at a rakish angle as if it too found standing in this Flemish mud too much of an effort. Those patches of grim reminders were everywhere along the road and gave mute testimony as to where the 'flower of the British Army' had gone. Then, too, one saw signs here and there, of where a soldier had 'gone West' perfectly calm but not collected. A chance shell had spoiled his dream of 'Blighty.'

Gangs of German prisoners were working on the roads scraping off the mud and pounding in fresh stone to make amends for their old-time destructiveness.

Several partially destroyed tanks of all sizes with the graves of the drivers and gunners close by gave proof of the dangers incurred in traveling in these moving forts.

Our route through this devastated land included the cities of Boesinghe, Polcappell, Langemarck, West Roosebeke, Hooglede, and a number of smaller places. The cities in the actual fighting area being entirely destroyed and the ones on the edges barely recongnizable as such.

Gitz—Pittham—Thielt

Just after nightfall, we pulled into the city of Gitz and were assigned to billets in an ex-brewery because there was nothing to brew, no one to brew it and artillery fire had wrecked the machinery. A well-placed shell had torn out the roof and dislocated some heavy shafting and it was expected that this would come tumbling down at any minute.

We were destined to stay at Gitz for five foodless days. The kitchen was with us all right but the amount of rations drawn was disheartening to look at save trying to feed the company with them.

The time was chiefly spent wishing for a meal, and in cleaning up the mule and wagon trains.

On October 28, we moved again, this time into the town of Pitthem. This proved to be a one night location with excellent billets in private houses and on the day following at one o'clock in the afternoon we moved toward the city of Thielt. About seven kilometers would cover this distance and we felt sure of another night's rest before the activity we felt sure was ahead.

Upon arriving at Thielt, the 73rd Brigade was billeted and after a wait of an hour or so along the streets the order came in to move on toward the front.

The word was then circulated that orders had changed and that we were to advance to a city near to the front and be billeted there.

The column halted midway between Denterghem and Olsene and supper of hot beans was served.

The *Chateau de Olsene*
Published June 16, 1919

At a turn in the road just before reaching Olsene the company became detached from the infantry column and nearly made the fatal error of marching straight into the enemy lines. After this mix-up had been straightened out, we proceeded to the cavalry pontoon bridge south of Olsene, crossed and were making our way toward the city when the Austrian gunners woke up and put two shells from their quick-firer into our midst.

The shells fell just at the bank of the river and in the midst of the headquarters of the infantry company we were following. When the confusion had cleared away it was found that they had suffered twelve dead and wounded. By the rules of war, we could not linger to help them but must needs move on. Just at the edge of the city the same gun made another attempt, missing us by the width of a hair.

Dodging our way through the streets to keep out of the way of the chance bullets whistling through now and then and the shells dropping among the buildings, we came at last to the *Chateau de Olsene*. Here was to be our billeting place that night.

The second and third platoons had been detached on the other side of the river and sent forward to relieve the French up in the line. The rest of the company tried to follow the infantry into the basement of the chateau but they informed us that they needed the room for themselves. The shelling grew heavier and at length Lieutenant Rew, company commander during the length of this engagement, hustled his men into the upper stories of the castle in an attempt to obtain some sort of cover.

Everyone was finally settled here about five AM and since we were dead tired, were soon asleep. About eight o'clock the enemy guns opened on the chateau and as each man gathered his possessions was let out the front door and told to make the gatehouse at the entrance of the grounds and to take cover in the cellar there. The change was soon made and sleep was resumed in the new location.

Runners brought up bread and molasses for the noon meal and after dark that evening a fine feed was carried up from the kitchen.

At ten o'clock that night, the First Platoon moved up to the railroad ahead of the chateau and mounted guns in reserve. Company headquarters also moved up nearby.

"Over" Once More

The barrage hour was 5:25 the morning of the 31st of October and as the first rockets went up the Company went over at the railroad while the other two platoons were in the midst of the infantry advance 800 meters ahead.

A number of casualties resulted in the first few minutes of the battle and the losses of that day in the Company were heavy. Lieutenant James Pease was wounded as was his runner, Private Edward Dyer, the first thing that morning. Sergeant Joseph D. Shultz assuming command of the platoon. First Sergeant Carl R. Hentz commanded the First Platoon throughout the drive and to whom belongs the credit for the efficient handling of his men with the result that the Scheldt River was crossed successfully and which goes down as one of the great military accomplishments of the war. Lieutenant Frank C. Leroy commanded the second platoon.

The close of the first day found the line advanced to the range of hills just ahead of Hutteghem and the attackers dug in waiting for dawn and a new start.

The causality list for this day included Corporal John S. Klinger, shrapnel; Lieutenant James Pease, bullet; Edward Dyer, bullet; Sergeant George Smith, shrapnel; Joseph Renato, shrapnel; Stanley Polglaze; Robert Johnson, bullet; Daniel Davidson, bullet; Tony Ruggerie, bullet; Arthur G. Brode, shrapnel; Private Rossnay; Charles Saunders, bullet; Ralph Cruzan, shrapnel and gas; Private Webber. All of these were seriously wounded.

Corporal Ivan Shanafelt, Private Clair Dunning, Eugene Everhart, Forest Pemberton, David Murphy and Sergeant Frederick Demmler paid for the gains of the day with their lives.

Private Raymond Steele

All of the hot action of that October morning wasn't in the immediate battle line either, as this account of the work of Private Steele will show.

"When the company went over the top, the mule train with re-serve bulk ammunition remained on the grounds of the *Chateau de Olsene*. The mules were tied to trees near the chateau while the men were quartered in an abandoned farm house six hundred meters distant.

During the German counter-barrage (about 7:30 AM) someone reported to Private Raymond Steele that his mule was loose. In spite of the heavy shelling, he set out at once. On arrival he found that a number of the animals had been killed by pieces of the flying H.E.s.

Realizing that the remainder might be saved by quick work in getting them under the cover of the nearby barn, he led them in one by one. Three were killed before he could get them away from the clump of trees. Private Steele barely escaped from being crushed under one of the animals when it fell.

Due to Private Steele's efforts, enough mules were saved to carry forward much needed ammunition to the company later on and to haul back the guns and equipment when they were relieved.

American Pluck

This first day Private Forest Pemberton fell mortally wounded, pierced through by enemy machine gun bullets.

Corporal Leo Damicon and others of his comrades offered aid to a nearby dressing station, but while they made preparations to carry him back he implored his companions to carry on. As Corporal Damicon proffered his assistance, the stricken man said, 'Get them, Leo. They got me.'

The stricken man died shortly after, in spite of the aid they sought to render him.

Another incident of this first day, and one which illustrates Ameri-can pluck and the way of the American in battle, is furnished by the conduct of Sergeant Fred Demmler.

As the Company went over the top near the Chateau, from posi-tions along the railroad tracks about 900 meters from the enemy front line, Sergeant Demmler commanded a squad of the First Platoon, whose guns were in support.

The platoon had little more than cleared the railroad when they were caught in the German counter barrage, shells falling everywhere and making any attempt at taking cover worse than useless. About seventy-five meters beyond the tracks, Demmler was struck by pieces of an exploding H.E. (high explosive) that fell in the midst of the squad he led.

Corporals Damicon and Marlett stopped and offered aid and assistance to a place where medical attention could be had, but to each his answer was the same, 'Keep on with the advance. They need everyone of you up ahead.'

Later Sergeant Demmler was found by runners returning to the Company and carried to the Olsene dressing station. Three days later, he died in the hospital.

The splendid record of this brave soldier has won the admiration of all who knew him.

Typical Hun Treachery
Published June 23, 1919

The second day of the advance the Germans were found to have drawn back and little or no resistance was encountered until the canal was reached toward evening.

A happening of this second afternoon gives a little insight on Hun methods.

"The Third Platoon was in action along the canal and the gunners had their pieces laid and were waiting for fire orders from the infantry commander. The enemy machine guns were stationed across an open field and the space of 'No Man's Land' between the two forces was occupied by an abandoned farmhouse. The entire front was under the eyes of the different commanders who were watching for the appearance of the enemy through their field glasses.

"At length, groups of men and women began to sally out of the house in the direction of the enemy's lines. The machine gun observers reported the occurrence to their gunners with the additional information that although the people appeared to be Belgians they were convinced that they were Germans dressed in cast-off civilian clothing. However, the infantry commander was of a different opinion and refused to allow them to use their guns.

"The day following the Huns repeated the trick. But they were prevented from making a success of the ruse for the gunners opened fire and put them to flight.

"The Germans had been using the house as a storage place for ammunition and had been driven to this subterfuge in order to supply themselves with much needed ammunition, camouflaging the belt boxes and Maxims as 'infants' in the arms of the 'women.' "

Crossing the Escaut

"The third day of the advance was continued in the vicinity of the river and during that night preparations were made for the attempt at crossing.

"Early in the morning of November 3, the order was given by the infantry commander whose company we were supporting to move forward to the river. Arriving there, it was found that it would be impossible to find sufficient cover to maintain a foothold, even along our side of the river. Investigation revealed that the only means of crossing the stream was by way of a narrow log, formerly used as a footbridge.

"The log furnished a risky means of crossing at best and the hazards were greatly increased by the continuous fire of the enemy. One H Company man was drowned in the swift waters of the river and I was saved from a similar fate only by the swift work of my comrades.

"The infantry company and our platoon 'dug in' on the opposite bank about 3:30 in the morning and later advanced about one kilometer, the latter positions fronting a large willow grove, that furnished ample protection from enemy observation.

"The last night up the platoon and infantry held out under a heavy enemy artillery barrage and in addition withstood an attack from the enemy aeroplanes dropping grenades and bombs and firing down the line of defense with their machine guns.

"During the entire action, the little command was flanked on three sides by the enemy and was exposed to direct fire from the enemy artillery.

"We were relieved on the night of the fourth of November by the French who, however, failed to cross the river and follow up the advantage we had gained. Three runners were sent to guide up the relieving troops, two from the infantry and one, Private Walter Keeter, from the machine gun platoon. The infantry runners were killed on the way to the infantry battalion headquarters and Private Keeter reached there severely wounded. This alone is proof of the German barrage fire."

The above account was furnished by Corporal Leon McGowan, at that time a gunner in one of the squads taking part in the action.

General DeGoute's Praise

Commenting on this achievement of the American arms, General DeGoute, commanding the Sixth French Army says:

"Attempting an operation of war of unheard audacity, the American units crossed the overflooded Escaut, under fire of the enemy and maintained themselves on the opposite bank of the river in spite of his counter attacks."

The gun teams taking part in the crossing of the river included the squads of Corporals Rice, Damicon, Barnard and Marlatt, First Sergeant Carl R. Hentz was platoon commander and to him belongs the credit for the leadership through which this achievement was carried out.

The casualties for these closing days included Privates Charles Barnes and Haggerman, Private Keeter, shrapnel; Private Clyde Reed, severely gassed; Privates Hare and Fossett, slightly wounded.

The City of Thielt

Coming out of the front line the Company again made their way to the Chateau de Olsene where they spent the daylight hours of the fifth and at four o'clock that afternoon made their way to the city of Thielt, arriving there about ten o'clock. Billets were provided in a hurry and the usual scurry was made for sleeping space.

Thielt proved to be a very attractive city and a pleasant place to rest up. A YMCA canteen gave good service and offered quite a variety of goods. Besides the city afforded any number of small shops that seemed to have prospered under the German rule and one could buy practically everything at prices that were quite reasonable when one considers the circumstances.

A British aviation field at the edge of the city proved to be quite an attraction and afforded no end of amusement.

A very beautiful building had housed the Trades Guilds of this thriving Belgian city and even in a state of ruin it presented on impressive appearance. The Belgian cities are noted for their guild halls and the one at Thielt had been one of the finest of the country. An immense auditorium had been one of the features of the hall and this part had escaped total ruin. This structure had been bombed while in use as a headquarters by the German occupational forces.

This city had in pre-war days boasted of a railway yard that in size compared with the American yards. It is impossible to give an idea of how little invaders had left untouched in this place. At the time of our departure from the city, the French had brought in a force of "tame" Huns and had them at work on the tracks leading into Thielt from the channel.

The War Ends

Saturday afternoon, November 9, we were again in motion toward the front. Sometime after dark that evening we pulled into the city of Deynze on the east bank of the Lys River.

We were put up for the night in an abandoned saw mill with no protection from the wind on four sides and very little roof. The battalion was to move before daybreak the next morning to the line not far distant.

Orders miscarried during the night, and the result was that we did not get under way until eight o'clock. We certainly moved when we did get on the road. In two hours, we had overtaken the rest of our forces and when we came up the orders were passed back that we were to halt for awhile and await developments.

The rolling kitchen was drawn over into a nearby turnip field and preparations for the noon meal were soon underway. The men settled themselves for a rest by the side of the road with an eye on the preparations going on about us.

Toward noon passing French troops imparted the tidings that "the war was finished." Knowing that the French celebrated the close of the war at least once a month, we paid little attention. A little later, an American dispatch rider confirmed the report and our hopes rose.

Armistice or no armistice, the preparation for the biggest battle of all time was going on with methodical precision. Fleets of armored cars rolled by toward the front. An endless chain of tanks followed in their wake. Artillery, light and heavy, was drawn up by horses, trucks and tractors. Caissons and lumber wagons passed and repassed on the road carrying their share of the thousands and thousands of shells to be used in the intense artillery preparation. Columns of blue-clad French hurried toward the line or made way for the khaki column moving in the same direction.

To our left and right the whistle of the enemy shells mingled with the bark of our field guns. The sharp rattle of machine guns on both sides gave proof that the dove of peace was an elusive bird and not easily trapped.

As evening wore on, an attempt was made to secure billets in nearby farm houses and shortly the company was housed comfortably to the discomfiture of the infantry units who were compelled to seek sleep in the ditches and fields in the immediate locality.

Dawn of November 11 brought sounds of a heavy barrage to our ears with the rumble of the field guns and the whistle of shells. The Allies had again attacked and in this particular locality had carried the Escaut completely for several miles and had taken several cities on the other bank.

The crash of shells and the rattle of the machine guns continued throughout the morning and small promise of the approaching close of hostilities could be gained from these. Speculation ran high as how the matter would end but more curiosity than interest was exhibited.

Eleven o'clock came at last and with it the first period of complete quiet that the Western Front had enjoyed for more than four years. The silence was almost uncanny. Every gun was silenced; the stream of traffic on the road had died down. Not a single plane winged its way overhead.

The troops up ahead told later of how the Huns came up out of their holes in the turnip fields and threw turnips at the Yanks who answered with a volley of colored flares and a mimic battle to good humor replaced the grim conflict of five minutes before.

Armistice night, the French soldiers in our locality made free with the juice of the grape and celebrated in first-class style. The cafés rang loud with music and many voices and now and then some celebrant would step to the door and fire a few rounds with his pistol or rifle, the bullets whistling around the neighboring houses and coming uncomfortably close to the thatched roofs.

In direct contrast to the Poilus, the Americans went quietly about their duties as if a war ended every day. Everyone welcomed the end but seemed unwilling to make a demonstration. Perhaps they feared it would all turn out to be a mistake and weren't taking any chances. The world did look just a bit better, the sun seemed a trifle brighter and everyone somewhat more cheerful.

A Long Hike
Published June 30, 1919

During the days following the armistice we enjoyed a touch of winter in Flanders and while the weather was not at all severe we thanked the fates that had closed the war. The wet ditches, sloppy roads and frosty nights made sitting around the cosy wood fires in the billets seem a veritable paradise when one thought that we might easily be working our way toward Germany under the most unpleasant conditions, to say the least.

The six days we remained here were spent in drilling and in taking long road hikes under full pack. We wondered why we were called upon to march endless practice miles with our packs on when the war was over. We soon learned the reason.

Just after dinner, November 17, we left the neighborhood of Huysse under full packs. The impression generally circulated was that we were bound for the Belgian capital city. On arriving at the town occupied by battalion headquarters, we were joined by the other companies of the battalion and then we learned definitely (or as definitely as anything is ever circulated in an army) that we were to proceed to Brussels and pass in grand review before the king of Belgium upon the occasion of his assuming his throne in the capital after holding his court in a town in Northern France for more than four years as a king without a kingdom.

Hiking until long after dark, we brought up in the village of Dikkle. We found that an infantry outfit had, as usual, appropriated every billet in the town and we were left out in the cold. A convenient stable or two provided a kind of shelter and the kitchen raked up a feed and all was well for the time.

Clearing out early the next morning, we marched to St. Lievens-Hauthem and billeted. This was a town of some size and boasted the first shops and cafés we had seen for some weeks. The monthly pay also arrived and it made a happy combination.

On the way here we had seen the evidence of the last days of the struggle in the region of the Escaut. Half finished pontoon bridges, rifle pits, burned houses, piles of ammunition, all told the story of the closing days of the greatest war.

During the German occupancy, St. Lievens-Hauthem had been the center of considerable American relief work among the civilian populace. On our arrival there, we were quartered in the disused school buildings of the convent. As a sign of their gratitude, the sisters of the convent prepared wafers for us on the evening of our last day there as a treat to the fellows quartered in the convent buildings.

Not only did they prepare wafers in abundance, but they actually coated them with sugar. To say that sugar was more precious than gems in war-ridden Belgium is putting it mildly. The depth of our appreciation of their kindness could only be felt for it could not be shown but the memory of the kindness of all the people of the little Belgian city will linger long in the minds of the Company and that of the women of the convent, especially.

After three days at St. Lievens, we were again underway, going back the way we had come and in the direction of the channel. A platoon had been selected from the entire battalion to honor the king and see Brussels at the same time. They were to join us at a later date after returning from "little Paris."

We stopped at Dikkle again for a night and this time spent the night in an abandoned schoolhouse. The next night was spent in the village of Astene, near Deynse on the Lys.

Thanksgiving Day

November 22, we arrived at Desselghem on the Lys after following the river down to Deynse. Our stay in Desselghem extended over a period of ten days. We drilled a little, hunted souvenirs, collected German money, some of the more adventurous ones helped raid the homes of several reputed pro-Germans and collected no little loot. Incidentally, we were given an opportunity to clean up for the first time in several weeks.

Last, but not least, we enjoyed Thanksgiving Day. The cooks put up a real honest-to-goodness dinner with all the holiday trimmings. Activity was suspended with the exception of church services by the battalion chaplain in the village church.

Crossing the Lys for the last time, we proceeded to the city of Iseghm and billeted in what had once been a large factory building used for manufacture of fibre brushes. The Germans had used it for billets and it was one of the filthiest places we encountered in all Europe. The Huns were never overly clean to say the least. Otherwise, the city was somewhat attractive. Tasty bits of pastry was on sale in the shops as well as other things of interest.

The next night was spent in our pup tents in the locality of what had formerly been the city of Staden. This city was located on the edge of the German line of defense and had been the target of artillery fire for the four years strife. Several mines had been exploded in the vicinity after the Germans had been driven out and we were warned not to investigate any strange contrivances wherever found. In spite of this, some of the curious went rabbit hunting and set a bomb off by tripping on a ground wire.

The route from Staden to Oostvlettern was through the horrible waste of No Man's Land described in an earlier chapter. We made the thirty-odd kilometers across this territory in a day and it was a relief to know it was behind us for the last time. This brought us just over the line into the Republic of France once more.

Cinq-Chemins (Five Roads) was the next stop. We remained here for ten days, spent mainly in the several cafés. Two places afforded musical instruments more noted for racket than music and dancing was the order of the day. Everyone danced. Visiting in the neighboring towns of Hondschoote and Rexpoede was popular.

Christmas Day at Eringham

December 17 the battalion was moved into the village of Eringham where we remained for a month. This place boasted of twelve houses in all. These included seven cafés, a church, two stores, a photographer and a mill. The winter was well underway and the mud was deep in all quarters.

The photographic establishment was managed by a young lady who was, to be conservative, winsome. During our stay, every man in the battalion, married and single, discovered it would be nice to send his likeness to the folks at home, and was moreover his duty to preserve his "phiz" as it appeared at this particular time.

Passes to visit Dunkerque was given out daily and many availed themselves of the opportunity to visit the channel port. Trucks hauled the sightseers to and from the city.

Christmas was a repetition of Thanksgiving largely. We were given a good feed, marched to church in the morning and given the rest of the day off. Cigarettes, tobacco, candy, etc. were distributed by the Red Cross, Knights of Columbus, YMCA, etc. and lucky bags donated by the Red Cross were drawn by chance and created a lot of fun. The Y furnished movies.

New Year's Day, the divisional show was given for the benefit of the battalion at the aviation field nearby. All in all, the month was well spent.

The battalion entrained at Esquelbec Station, January 15, and northern France knew us no more. Two days later, we unloaded at Le Hutte in the Le Mans area. Here, we were joined by a number of returned casualties from different hospitals. Thirteen had rejoined the company at Desselghem.

St. Remy du Plain

A hike of twelve kilometers brought us to St. Remy du Plain. This was a clean little place and our billets were halfway decent. There was considerable speculation as to when we would pull for the coast but no one seemed to know.

Several trips to the delouser at Fresnay-sur-Sarthe served to rid the battalion of the troublesome "cootie." The paper work was inspected and efforts were made to get the individual equipment in order and up to requirements. Slim Anderson "issued and issued" in spite of all he could do to stop the flow of new clothing, etc.

The food situation was acute as usual but practically everyone had a little money and the cafés put up rather good "feeds," so no one starved.

While here the leave area of St. Malo in the north coast was opened to the battalion and practically everyone took advantage of the seven-day vacation at the expense of the government. This included a trip to the famous Mont St. Michel.

Leaving St. Remy February 17, we moved to Mezieres and there prepared the sailing lists, etc., attendant upon sailing. March 1 we hiked to Beaumont and entrained to Brest, our seaport.

Home Again

On arriving at Brest Sunday evening, March 2, the battalion was promptly detrained, led to a large troop kitchen and fed and then marched up the steep slope leading through the city and out to the huge embarkation camp.

What a contrast the place presented to the Brest camp of nine months before. The old Pontanezan barracks had been surrounded for miles with barracks and tents and the camp that had been taxed to take of a small brigade the previous summer accommodated a small army easily. The camp was bright with myriad electric lights, replacing the candle light we had used in the old barracks. The romantic glamor of the old Napoleonic days had quite departed and American efficiency had taken its place.

The battalion was located in tents in the midst of the great camp and assigned to a troop kitchen for rations. One of these kitchens were quite able to feed a regiment in less than no time it seemed. Most of the succeeding days were filled with endless details for work about the camp and included calls for men to perform every kind of labor from chopping wood to coaling a battleship.

After a thorough delousing, we moved into a "clean camp" in barracks and there awaited our sailing orders. Pay day came around and "white money" was the medium of exchange once more. Dollar bills ceased to be a luxury or a part of one's souvenir collection.

Tuesday, March 11, we stepped out of our barracks, shouldered our packs and hiked to the docks where a lighter took us out beyond the breakwater and loaded us on the U.S.S. *Huntington*. We had carefully scraped the dust of France from our "hobs" and were, to say the least, relieved to be on way westward.

A little after eight the following day, the *Huntington* steamed out of the harbor and we had entered upon the first of our thirteen days of sea voyaging. The trip was over the southern route and was pleasant in every sense. The days were spent on the deck and with the exception of a day out of New York, no rough weather was encountered notwithstanding that it was at the close of the winter and a stormy season at best.

Now, as we steam into the harbor of New York, past the light ship and the coast patrol boats, and strain our eyes for the first sight of Mother Liberty, we will leave the company to enjoy the welcome accorded them by the Ohio delegation headed by the mayor of New York and Youngstown, when they shall have come alongside in their police tug, for our European travels are at an end.

Postscript

Sadly there is never an end and war leaves scars that take a long time to heal. Whether they be in the heart or war borne on the body, they go on and on.

The Ravenna Republican:
Monday, December 20, 1920
Wound Causes Vet Months of Trouble
Private Arthur Brode Spends Two Years in
Hospital as Result of Wound

Ex-private Arthur Brode, formerly of Company C 136th Machine Gun Battalion, Ravenna's fighting unit in the World War, returned to the home of his parents, Mr. and Mrs. James Brode, of Beechwood, last week, having spent nearly a year in the Public and Walter Reed Hospitals at Washington, D.C., as a result of a wound received on October 31, 1918, while in Belgium.

Brode was struck in the chest and on the hip by part of the high explosive shell that killed Clair Dunning, of Ravenna, and Ivan Shanafelt of Kent. The hip wound healed rapidly, and has never given him much bother, but the chest injury has kept him under medical care most of the time since he was struck.

He returned to the States just one day ahead of Company C, in the hospital. He was sent to Camp Sherman, Chillicothe, Ohio, for treatment, and remained there in the hospital until August 1919, when he was transferred to Fort McPherson, Georgia. In January, 1920, it was believed that the wound had healed, and he was given an honorable discharge from the service.

Brode then went to Washington, D.C., where he intended to visit his sister, but had hardly arrived there when his wound broke open again, and he was sent to the public health hospital, and later transferred to Walter Reed, where many veterans are recuperating. He was finally operated on and the piece of shell in his chest removed, and since then he has been getting gradually better. He left the hospital last week.

Brode enlisted at Ravenna, being in the van of those who lined up to organize Company M Tenth Ohio Infantry, which later became Company C, 136th Machine Gun Battalion.

∘   ∘   ∘

Each Memorial Day and Veteran's Day let us pause to remember those gave all they had in whatever way that we might be free. We owe them a legacy we can never fully repay.

Index

Abel, Clark, 5
Adair, James, 31
Adio, Jas., 36
Alexander, Alfred, 5
Anderson, Harold A. (W.), 5, 10, 15, 27, 29, 37, 45, 59, 64, 77, 97
  Melvin G. (C.), 10, 15, 27, 36
  "Slim", 205
Andrews, Harold W., 9

Baldwin, Charles Henry, 9, 10, 15, 27, 37, 58
Ballist, Charles C., 25
Barnard (Bernard), John T., 198
  Judge, 68, 69
Barnell (played cornet), 82
Barnes, Charles, 198
Barrett, Ford, 58
Barry, General, 29
Bartholomew, Howard R., 11, 15, 27, 36, 145
Bath, Raymond, 186
Batsch, Charles, 35
Baugh, Harold, 37
  Howard, 39
Baxter, Charles H., 27, 59
  Clarence A., 10, 15, 36, 68, 74
Beckley, W. J., 2, 12
Bender, Clyde, 130
Bernard, John, 39
Bibb, Sophie, 54
Bible, Howard L., 88
Bienville, 54

Blieu, Lewis C., 5, 9, 10, 15, 27, 37, 165
Block, Clifford, 64
Blumenschein, Herman, 131
Boak (Boke), Harold P., 15, 27, 36, 68, 86, 89, 147
Bosworth, Thomas, 36, 39, 130, 147
Boy Scouts, 20
Boyd, Lawrence S. (R.), 10, 15, 27, 31, 37
Bradley, Mrs. Mary, 94
Brockett, Norman A. (H.), 15, 27, 36
Brode, Arthur G., 10, 15, 27, 37, 59, 130, 132, 146, 194, 207, 208
  Mr. and Mrs. James, 132, 207
Buck, Amos, 82, 96
Byers, Charles R., 27, 36, 51
  John R., 5, 10, 27, 36, 65, 74, 81
  Fred (Mayor), 2

Caesar, 154
Cannavino (Cannivino), Mark, 10, 16, 27, 36, 59, 74, 82, 131
Cannon, Clell C., 16, 27, 36
Carter, Joseph F., 5, 10, 16, 27, 29, 36, 65, 68
Chambers, Floyd (J.) (S.), 5, 9, 10, 16, 27, 37
Chickeno, Amelio, 16, 27, 36, 82
Christy, Captain, 14
Church of Christ (First Christian Church), 29, 138, 144
Cincinnati Reds, 80

Clamcy, Rev. Fr. C.J., 94
Clark, George, 8, 10, 16, 27, 31
Cliff (Cliffe), Lieutenant Earl W.,
    8, 14
Clinger, J.B., 25
Cobb, Irvin S., 187
Coburn Minstrel Troupe, 72, 73
Cole, Joseph A. (R.), 5, 9, 10, 16,
    27, 36, 59
Conaway, Charles M., 5, 9, 10, 16,
    27, 40, 43, 47, 50, 53, 57, 67,
    72, 76, 80, 82, 84, 87, 90, 95,
    113, 114, 148, 180, 185
Congregational Church, 15, 30
Conway, William (Bill), 29, 36, 44,
    51, 73, 77, 82, 146
Cook, Elmer (Bill), 29
Cope, Charles A. (R.), 5, 7, 9, 10,
    12, 16, 19, 26, 36, 37, 44, 48,
    51, 63, 69, 74, 77, 94
Coughlin, Private, 64
    Mr. and Mrs. J.T., 64
Coverdale, George, 131
Creese, Ezra K., 27, 37, 46, 68, 173
Creque, Frank G. (C.), 10, 16, 27,
    37, 58, 59, 65, 131
Cristy, Major, 14, 41
Cruzan, Ralph, 194
Cummins, Mark, 65

Damicon, Leo A., 10, 16, 27, 37, 82,
    92, 130, 151, 172, 195, 196,
    198
D.A.R. (Daughters of the American
    Revolution), 29
Davey, Congressman M.L., 133,
    135
Davidson, Daniel, 194
    George E., 10, 16, 27, 36, 83

Davis, Claude M., Jr., 16, 27, 65,
    145, 147, 185
    Jefferson, 54
    Lynn A., 25
Dawley, Lieutenant Arthur, 58
De Angelis (De Angelio)
    (Deangles), Benjiman
    (Benjamin) (Ben), 10, 16, 27,
    36
DeGoute, General, 198
Demmler, Frederick, 130, 172,
    173, 194, 195, 196
Densmore, Charles R., 25, 27
Dickens, Frederick, 10, 16, 27, 31,
    36
Diezman, Arthur L., 7, 9, 10, 16,
    27, 37
Ditzman, Rollin F., 25
Dunning, Claire (Clair S.), 5, 9, 10,
    16, 27, 36, 54, 59, 73, 113, 127,
    130, 145, 173, 194, 207
    Mr. and Mrs. George M., 127
Dustin, Lynn H., 27, 37, 65, 98
Dustman, Dewey A., 10, 16, 27, 37,
    85, 131
Dyer, Edward F., 10, 16, 27, 37,
    130, 194

Eastock, John, 69
Elgin, Carl H., 36, 73, 83, 147
    Elmer, 73
    Frank (W.) (K.) (Sergeant), 5, 10,
    16, 27, 36, 44, 73, 85, 147
Elks, 145
Eunello, Joseph, 130
Everhart, Eugene, 194

Fairchild, and Son, 28
Farnsworth, General, 130, 146
Farse, Lieutenant, 92

Ferry (Ferny), Frank W., 11, 16, 27, 31, 36, 147

Filiatraut, Clark F.W., 60

Fisher, Harry C., 25, 27, 36
John, 11

Fleishman (Fleshman), George P., 16, 27, 36, 66, 68, 81, 82, 86, 96, 97, 131, 173, 186

Floyd, Otto S., 16, 27, 37

Foch, General, 108

Fossett, Private, 198

Francies, C.R., 134, 137, 138

Frank, Chester, 5

Fulton, William D. (Secretary of State), 60

Galbraith, Colonel, 90, 92

Gano, Charlie, 73, 74

G.A.R. (Grand Army of the Republic), 15, 21, 24

Gaston, General, 87, 90

George, Kennerdell E. (Kennerdel) (Kennerdal), 10, 16, 27, 36, 51, 74, 147, 173

Gilbert, Leon K., 25

Gilion, Thomas G., 27

Gilson, Edward J., 27, 37, 74, 82, 83, 94
Mrs. Edward, 94
Thomas G., 11, 16
John H., 27

Gless, Carl A., 16, 27, 36, 89

Goodyear, Emmett, 5
Ethel (Mrs. Fred), 122

Grace Episcopal Church, 21

Gray, Clarence, 5
Mr. and Mrs. H.E., 101
Lee M., 186
William F. (W.P.), 5, 9, 10, 16, 27, 37, 82, 94, 101

Haas (Hase), Corporal Harold, 37, 51, 65, 97, 147
Kennith M. (Kenneth), 10, 16, 27, 37, 147

Haggerman, Private, 198

Hallabaugh (Hollabaugh) (Holabaugh), Clifford F., 10, 16, 27, 37, 75

Hanselman, S.F., 7

Hare, Edward A., 131, 198

Harris, Adj. Gen., 136

Hartman, D.G., 28

Hasely, Private, 58

Hauger, Rev. Charles H., 8, 12, 13, 21

Hawk, Ralph E., 16, 27, 31, 36, 147

Haymaker, Miss Elizabeth, 139

Hays, Stewart B., 88

Hazen, Mr. and Mrs. L.L., 29

Heath, Jessie M., 96
Mr. and Mrs. Ivan, 96

Henderson, Governor, 84, 85

Hentz, Carl R., 25, 27, 51, 113, 130, 171, 188, 194, 198
Raymond, 36

Herts, Sergeant, 74

Hill, Mr. and Mrs. Frank, 122
Leon, 39, 74, 89, 122
Norman, 122
Raymond L. (Elwood), 27, 37, 74, 89, 122, 145, 186

Hobbs, Rossiter, 130

Hoff, Sergeant Arthur E., 7, 18, 29, 36

Hoffman, P.V., 88

Hoover, Herbert, 187

Horne, William F. (E.) (Will), 5, 9, 10, 16, 27, 37
Walter, 37

Howard, Colonel, 58

Hubbard, Royce R., 27, 48, 51, 64, 68, 74
Hubbell, Mr. and Mrs. Charles, 93
  Harold (L.), 5, 7, 9, 10, 16, 19, 26, 36, 37, 41, 44, 45, 48, 67, 69, 77, 86, 93, 181, 186
Hudgins, Sergeant, 64, 65
Huff, 68
Hutchins, Dr., 68

Jackson, General Andrew, 72
  Wallace, N., 10, 16, 27, 97
  William, 37
Jacobsen (Jacobson) (Jacobus), Berger H., 10, 16, 27, 36, 186
James, Nicholas (Nick), 9, 16, 27, 37
Jenson, Nick, 5
Jewels, Sam, 36
John, Gilbert C. (A.), 25, 27, 31, 36
Johnson, Mayor, 133
  Robert, 194
Jones, John H., 10, 16, 27, 36, 68, 147
  Joseph (Sheriff) and Mrs., 99, 100, 101, 117
  LeRoy (Roy), 5, 9, 10, 17, 27, 37, 65, 74, 99, 100, 101, 117, 119, 130
  Paul (Corporal), 58
  Thomas Edward, 25, 27, 36, 54, 65, 147, 186
  William, 101

Kaiser, Wilhelm, 4, 58
Keeter, Walter J., 5, 9, 10, 17, 27, 37, 146, 180, 198
Kelley (Kelly), Robert, 36
Kennedy, John C., 27, 37, 74, 89
Keys (Keyes), Chester, 25, 27, 36, 51, 124, 126, 172, 179
  Lionel (Mr. and Mrs.), 124
Kick, Luther M., 10, 17, 27, 31, 37
Klingler (Klinger), John S., 27, 130, 194
Klingman, Private J.L., 122
Knapp, James F., 11, 17, 27, 37, 60
Knights of Columbus, 99, 204
Krieble (Kreible), Emerson R. (P.), 5, 8, 11, 17, 27, 37, 61, 89, 104, 105, 120, 130
  Mr. and Mrs. P.E. (P.K.), 61, 120

Lackey (Lockey), John W. (M.), 11, 17, 27, 82, 96, 97, 147, 181, 185
Lafalce (Lafalee), Sam, 37, 180
Lane, Carl, 58
Larcus, James (Jim), 27, 31, 36
Lauver (Lawver), Ray (Roy), 11, 17, 27, 36, 65
Law, Ruth, 88
Lawrence, Major N.C., 21
Leffel (Musician), 56
Leroy, Charles V., 27, 37 82, 89, 94
  Frank C., 146, 194
  James N., 25
  James (Mr. and Mrs), 94
Lincoln, President, 6, 13, 21
Lindsay (Lindsey), Robert J. (C.), 11, 17, 27, 42, 74, 86
  Mr. and Mrs. E.C., 42
Littrell, Mr., 29
Lock, John, 5
Logan, Major John A., 21, 45, 146, 148, 149, 154
Long, Fred A. 25, 55
  Raymond E. (Ray), 7, 8, 11, 17, 27, 36, 51
Loomis, H.R., 2, 3

Love, Major, 1, 14, 19
Lutz, William B., 17, 27, 93
  Willis E., 36, 93, 147
  Mrs. Willis, 93

Maccarone (Macherone)
    (Maccherone), Frank, 25, 27,
    36
Mahan, Freeman, 32, 33, 35, 58
  Hugh, 32, 35, 58
  Mr. and Mrs. W.H., 32
Mann, General W.A., 31
Marine Italian Band, 12, 144
Marlatt, Corporal Felix, 130, 196,
    198
Marsh, Jesse L., 11, 17, 27, 37, 48,
    94
  Shearold L. (Shirl), 11, 17, 27,
    36, 48, 94
Martin, Grant A., 173
Mattherwson, Christy, 80
Maurer, Edgar W., 100
Maxwell, John T., 130
McCay, Them (Thereon) (Theron),
    94, 96, 173
McCord, Capt. Wm., 53, 86
McGowan, Leon, 198
McIlwain, Rev. Francis, 20, 21, 24
McIntosh, David (Post), 15, 21, 144
McKeever (McKeefer) George W.,
    11, 17, 27, 37
McMaken, General, 87
McMullen, Charlie, 81, 82, 186
McReed, Clasto, 37
Meredith (Merydith), Raleigh K.,
    27, 31, 36, 147
Methodist First Episcopal Church,
    8, 12, 21, 138, 144
Meyers, William F., 11, 17, 146

Miller, Maxwell M., 11, 17, 27, 37,
    65, 86, 147
  Sam, 183
Minnick (Minnich), Wilbur C.
    (Wilber), 11, 17, 27, 36, 59, 74,
    146, 185
Moff, Frank, 36
Moncey, Francis, 7
Moniet, Mary, 94
Montigney, Henry, 5
Moon, George H., 11, 17, 27, 36,
    80, 86, 147
Moore, Walter J., 36
  Walter O., 8, 11, 17, 27
  Willis, 5
Moreland, Chester C., 140
Morgan, John, 5
Mosier, Leon, 11, 17, 27, 31, 36,
    145
Mott, H. Harold, 5, 9, 11, 17, 27,
    36, 66, 69, 79
Murphy, David N. (M.), 5, 17, 27,
    36, 116, 145, 194
  Frank, 131
  Mr. and Mrs. George M., 116
  Syndey, 130
Murray, Frank D., 173
Muster, Leon, 8
Myers, George W., 11, 17, 27, 36,
    40, 45, 49, 66, 68
  William, 27, 36, 147, 185

Napoleon, 155
Neikirk, E.D., 1, 3, 7, 11
Nelle, Herbert, 7
Norman, Quay, 75
North, Second Lieutenant John
    K., 171

Old Northwest Chapter, 29

Palm, Edward R., 25
Parham, John, 20
Parker, Cleon L., 27, 37
　Major, 57
Parsons (Parson), George W., 5, 9,
　11, 17, 27, 37, 131
Pease, "Jim" James, 188, 194
Pemberton, Forest C. (Forrest), 25,
　27, 36, 66, 89, 130, 145, 194,
　195
Pershing, John J., 177
Piazzi (Piazz), Ben, 25, 27, 36
Pierce, Franklin (Battalion
　Commander), 146
Polglaze (Polglase), Henry S., 25,
　27
　Stanley, 37, 194
Post's Band, 144
Price, Earl C., 11, 17, 27, 37, 59,
　67, 74
　Captain, 153
Puffer, Harry S., 11, 17, 27, 31,
　36, 145

Raier, Albert, 131
Rainbow Division, 31, 39, 145, 147
Ravenna City Band, 12, 20, 144
Reale, Jas., 36
Red Cross, 20, 29, 139, 150, 151,
　204
Redmond, Bert and Mrs., 110, 129,
　133, 134, 136, 138, 144
Reed, Clyde, 37, 65, 74, 131, 198
Reigle, John, 36
Renato (Ronato), Joseph, 9, 11, 27,
　36, 194
Rew, Lieut. Clyde, 45, 67, 76, 77,
　166, 168, 179, 181, 182, 186,
　193
Rex, 69

Rice, Alva B., 9, 11, 17, 27, 37, 86,
　130, 198
　William, 86
Rich, Thomas, 131
Richardson, Eugene, 25
Richison, William, 85, 130
Robertson, Archie M., 5
Robinson, Harold, 5
Robison, Judge E.F., 2, 5
Rock, Jack, 82
　John, 11, 17, 27, 36
Roller, Lester H., 37, 96
　Peter, 39
Rossnay, Private, 194
Rosso, Angelo, 130
Rufi, Joseph (Joe), 11, 17, 27, 36, 82
Ruggieri (Ruggiere) (Ruggerie),
　Tony, 5, 11, 17, 27, 36, 85, 194
Runyon, Harold, 130
Ryan, James, 186

Salvation Army, 189
Sanders (Saunders), Charles H., 27,
　37, 65, 86, 194
　George, 131
　Howard C., 25
Sawyer, Bennett J. (Ben), 11, 17,
　27, 31, 36, 147
Schweitzer, Fritz, 78
Shanafelt, Ivan W., 11, 17, 27, 36,
　93, 98, 107, 145, 147, 168,
　194, 207
　Mr. and Mrs. W.A., 98
Shanley, Gerald E. (Gerold), 11, 17,
　27, 36, 74
Sharp, C.R., 134
Shultz (Schultz), Elmer E. Jr., 17,
　27, 36, 97, 129
　Joseph D. (Joe), 17, 27, 36, 51,
　130, 194

Siddall, Kudge I.T., 2, 37, 71, 99,
    100, 106, 109, 115, 129
  Kingdon T., 2, 3, 12, 18, 19, 26,
    28, 29, 31, 36, 37, 40, 41, 44,
    45, 47, 48, 49, 51, 54, 55, 59,
    64, 65, 69, 71, 76, 77, 78, 82,
    99, 100, 106, 107, 109, 113,
    115, 118, 128, 129, 137, 138,
    144, 146, 171, 174, 178, 179,
    181, 182, 186
Simpson, Walter A., 11, 17, 27, 59,
    68, 76, 86, 89, 147
Skilton, William B., 11, 17, 27, 36,
    131
Slavin (Slaven), William J., 11, 18,
    27, 36, 70, 118
Smith, George H. (E.), 11, 18, 27,
    37, 74, 88, 130, 194
  Kenner, 89
  Mechanic, 88
  Roland R., 88
  William B. (R.), 11, 18, 27, 37,
    74, 131
Snell, Pvt. Ralph, 47
  Sergeant, 47
Sodaker, Victor, 186
Spade, Christopher, 37
Spangler, Michael, 27, 31, 36, 147
  Mitchel, 25
Sprecht (Specht), Samuel C., 9, 11,
    18, 27
Steele, Raymond, 194, 195
Stidsen, C.B., 69
  John, 18
Stockman, David, 110
Strayer, Herbert, 27, 36
  Hubert C. (Huber G.) 11, 18,
    147, 186

Summers, Leslie "Smoke", 97
  Raymond A., 9, 11, 18, 27, 37,
    58, 97, 130
Sutherland, Cyril H., 146
Swager, William, 58
Swartout, Howard E. (Harold), 18,
    27, 37, 68, 74, 130, 147
Swartz, Dennis, 25, 27, 36, 81, 147
Szekula, Frank, 5

Terrell, Virgil, 25
Theiss (Theis), Ervin (Erwin), 86,
    96
Thompson, Hubert (Herbert E.), 5,
    8, 11, 18, 27, 37, 74
  Walter A., 37
Tinder, Wallace, 185
Titanic, 21
Tousley, Clyde E.T., 149
Treat, Charles G., 84, 85, 90
Treavitts, W.J., 96
Trexler, William (Bill) (H.) (F.), 5,
    9, 11, 18, 27, 36, 65, 70, 74,
    81, 118
Trixie, 58, 69
Turner, Mr. (from Mantua), 7

Valento, Frank, 27, 36
Vitzthum, Carl, 37

Walter Reed Hospital, 207
Washington, President, 21
Watkins, Don, 97
Watters, John, 29
Webber, C.C., 2, 3
  Private, 194
Weideman (Weidman), Cletus J.,
    11, 18, 27, 31, 36, 147
Weiss, Ralph J., 25
Weldy, Hiram Bayne, Jr., 18, 27, 37

Weybrecht, Col. C.C., 40, 41, 45
White, George, 97
Wicks, Capt., 92
Wilhelm, Kaiser, 3, 58, 110, 170
Williams, Harvey G., 75, 82
Wilson, President, 6, 28, 92
Wilt, Harry, 18, 27, 37, 147
Women's Relief Corps (W.R.C.),
   15, 20, 21, 24, 29, 144

Wood, Adjutant General, 19
Wright, Earl S., 36

Yeend, Mr. and Mrs. J.C. 39
   Robert W. (N.) (K.), 9, 11, 18,
      24, 27, 29, 36, 39, 47, 50, 51,
      55, 58, 65, 74
Y.M.C.A., 44, 99, 102, 153, 155,
   158, 173, 199, 204